THE BIRTH OF
MATHEMATICS
IN THE AGE OF
PLATO

THE BIRTH OF
MATHEMATICS
IN THE AGE OF
PLATO

FRANÇOIS LASSERRE

AMERICAN RESEARCH COUNCIL
Larchmont, N. Y.

Library of Congress Catalog Card Number: 65-16847
Manufactured in the United States of America

Gift

Contents

Foreword

No series devoted to the history of science can leave out an event of such importance for the development of Western thought as the birth of theoretical mathematics. Without embarking on a much larger book, however, it is impossible to touch on all the discoveries that led, over more than thirty centuries, from the invention of numerals to the advent of algebra. I have therefore decided to select from this very long period the first point at which mathematics was converted from a science of concrete things to one based on abstractions. This is not an arbitrary decision: inasmuch as mathematicians today regard their discipline as a collection of theories rather than an accumulation of practical knowledge, the transition from the concrete to the abstract is surely the most important moment in the history of mathematics. The 'moment', it is true, extended over several generations, but it passed through a crucial phase in the quarter of a century which followed the introduction of mathematics into the programme of studies at Plato's Academy. At this point those fundamental ideas were defined in which a present-day mathematician can still recognize his own modes of thought. So this modest work seeks to explain the birth of modern mathematics by describing the progress of mathematical thought at the time of Plato.

In such a restricted chronological framework every minute is precious. So I have felt justified in focussing the reader's attention, sometimes at length, on every one of the steps that led to the advent of theoretical mathematics. I have in this way tried to bring alive before his eyes the intellectual activities of the ancient mathematicians, rather than to draw up a balance sheet of their researches, however impressive that might be. I hope the reader will bear this in mind. The same considerations have led me not to stress the technical aspects of their discoveries but rather to pinpoint the principal ideas which guided them. In fact, after pondering Euclid's famous reply to King Ptolemy on being asked how he could learn geometry easily—'In mathematics there are no short cuts, even for a king'—I have tried to do justice to Ptolemy rather than to Euclid, and to awaken the reader's philosophical curiosity rather than engage him in logical exercises.

Finally, I have attempted to present to the reader the very texts in which the thoughts of the ancient mathematicians are expressed. Whether they are explaining the principles of their science or whether they are demonstrating new theorems, only the texts written in their own hands make their patterns of thought immediately intelligible. As most of these texts appear in little-known treatises or extracts, often difficult to obtain either in translation or in the original, I have taken the opportunity of compiling from them an anthology which is, as far as I am aware, the first of its kind, and I hope therefore that it will be of some service.

Thanks to the works of Sir Thomas Heath, the English-speaking public possesses invaluable documentation on Greek mathematics. I owe more to them than I can say. I should like in particular to acknowledge that, with the kind permission of the publishers, I have taken translations of several Greek quotations from the following works:

Aristarchus of Samos: the ancient Copernicus. Clarendon Press (Oxford, 1913).

A History of Greek Mathematics, vol. I. Clarendon Press (Oxford, 1921).

The Thirteen Books of Euclid's Elements, 3 vols. Cambridge University Press, 2nd ed. 1925 (reprinted 1956).

Mathematics in Aristotle. Clarendon Press (Oxford, 1949).

FOREWORD

I am equally indebted to Dr Stephen Toulmin, not only for supervising the translation of this rather intricate text, but also for much encouragement during its preparation and for valuable advice subsequently.

F. LASSERRE

EDITOR'S NOTE

This translation has been prepared by Miss Helen Mortimer, with the assistance of Mrs Maureen Mestheneos and Mrs Alice Smol.

S.E.T.

I

What Is Mathematics?

Ask a philosopher 'What is philosophy?', or a historian 'What is history?', and they will have no difficulty in giving an answer. Neither of them, in fact, can pursue his own discipline without knowing what he is searching for. But ask a mathematician 'What is mathematics?': he may justifiably reply that he does not know the answer, but that this does not prevent him from doing mathematics. What is the reason for this difference?

A neat explanation springs immediately to mind—that in philosophy, as in history, the end defines the means; whereas in mathematics the means define the end. If one were to make available to the historian, outside his own science, all the methods developed by sciences auxiliary to history, but were to deny him the documents on which to carry out his research, he would be condemned to idleness. By the same token, if one were to imagine a philosopher who never asked himself a question of any kind, it would be impossible for him to 'practise philosophy'. But put a mathematician in the historian's place, and he would need only to invent some problems in order to be as busy as he could wish. Again, put him in the situation of the philosopher: if he is so lacking in imagination that he cannot find a problem to solve for himself, he will still have the chance of following through *ad infinitum* the implications of his predecessors' discoveries.

If this explanation satisfies us for the time being, because (for example) it seems to suggest that mathematics has no well-defined goal, while other sciences do have such a goal, it goes no further towards answering the question we posed at the outset: What is mathematics? For centuries, undoubtedly, the collection of sciences covered by this term was not isolated from the multitude of activities of the *homo faber*. And when it was eventually given a name of its own it is very unlikely that anyone took the trouble at the time to give a formal definition of it. Asking questions about the nature of a science is a typically modern preoccupation. In the particular case of mathematics, such a question could not be asked before it had become the theoretical science that it still is today. As long as arithmetic was used only in book-keeping by tradesmen and tax-collectors, and geometry solely for measuring land and buildings, nobody thought of determining their nature or their ultimate object. On the other hand, once divorced from their practical applications, these same disciplines created a philosophical problem, and since that time this problem has never ceased to trouble the consciousness of mathematicians. So the transition from primitive mathematics to modern mathematics is marked far less by a straightforward displacement of practical preoccupations by theoretical ones, than by the emergence of a new anxiety: that of giving a meaning to these preoccupations.

This anxiety had not been felt previously either by the Babylonians or by the Egyptians. The Greeks were the first to experience it, and the first to seek to resolve it. This could be shown here immediately by considering the different definitions or classifications of the mathematical sciences which they have left us. One would see, gradually taking shape, the characteristics with which we are now familiar. But the modernism of the trends there evident will appear better by comparison, after a rapid glance at some of the definitions which have best expressed the views of modern mathematicians. For this reason, we may begin with these last, and return only afterwards to the origins of the problem.

From the Renaissance to the present day, mathematics has been regarded as the science of the relations uniting certain so-called 'mathematical' entities. This conception, inherited from antiquity, has so seldom been questioned that it has generally been felt useless to restate it by means of a formal definition. Among philosophers, particularly, this conception has been fundamental, and it is one of them, Auguste Comte, who stressed it:

> The exact definition of this science consists in saying that one is concerned throughout to compare magnitudes, according to the exact relations which exist between them.

Although they are unanimous on this point, mathematicians do not agree about the nature of the entities with whose relations mathematics is concerned. The above quotation refers to them as 'magnitudes' because the Renaissance, adopting a term devised by Eudoxus of Cnidus, the most celebrated mathematician of Plato's time, defined them in this way. But the nineteenth century questioned this definition and put forward several others. In fact the progress of sciences such as astronomy and physics was then opening new horizons for mathematicians, at the same time that the non-Euclidean geometry of Gauss, Lobatchevsky and Riemann was upsetting the fundamental notions in which they had believed. It seemed possible, therefore, that mathematics was actually going to bring within its scope entities quite different from those it had considered hitherto. Hence the numerous attempts, during the second half of the nineteenth century, and throughout the twentieth century right up to the present day, to give definitions of 'mathematical entities'. And yet, as we shall see, these definitions do not depart from the two contrasted conceptions whose principles antiquity distinguished once for all, and which can be summed up in the phrases: 'real objects', and 'imaginary objects'. Twenty-five years of thought and discussion in Plato's Academy sufficed to delimit the field of mathematics in all its breadth.

Let us now examine the texts which reflect the most widely divergent ideas of modern times. The definition of mathematics as the science of 'real objects', which goes back to Plato himself, is the one to which Auguste Comte refers in the text quoted above. It dominated Western thought until his time and was formulated very concisely on several occasions. Let us take as an example an Encyclopaedist, the philosopher and mathematician, d'Alembert:

> Mathematics is the science which concerns itself with the properties of magnitude, insofar as this can be measured and calculated.

The opposing conception, which was asserted at the very heart of the Academy as early as Plato's time, has in the early twentieth century found its most brilliant supporter in Bertrand Russell, the originator of mathematical logic. This conception prompted him to put forward the following definition:

> Mathematics is the science concerned with the logical deduction of consequences from the general premises of all reasoning.

More recent accounts have suggested a synthesis of these two attitudes. Their authors, without denying that the objects of mathematical analysis may equally well be either concrete realities or hypotheses of the imagination, are seeking for the point of contact between these two kinds of entity, and are attempting to understand the principles governing their association. This study has resulted in various formulations, of which one of the most striking—and the most recent (1948) —comes from the Bourbaki group:

> Mathematics manifests itself as a reservoir of abstract forms—the mathematical structures—and it turns out that certain aspects of experiential reality model themselves on some of these forms.

The men of antiquity, who left no such formulation, probably did not even envisage the possibility of a synthesis. But they did provide the terms for it, and thus served—in however distant and overlooked a way—as the direct inspiration of contemporary thought. In the 'abstract forms' of contemporary mathematicians we recognize the axioms of Euclid's predecessors, and in the 'aspects of experiential reality' Plato's mathematical universe. The current definitions employ a more subtle and exact terminology than the ancient ones, but they embody the same ideas. In mathematics, as in so many other fields of thought—history, philosophy, medicine, literature, the plastic arts—Greek antiquity succeeded, for the first time, in formulating the essential questions correctly, and in tracing their possible solutions in broad outline. In this sense, then, it was truly the cradle of modern mathematics.

Historical data

An adequate number of texts, for the most part easy to interpret, give us all the information we require about the development of ideas during the period in question. Before studying them more closely let us first recall certain facts and dates.

In 385 B.C., when he was about forty-five years old, Plato opened in Athens the school which was soon to bear the name 'Academy'. In less than twenty years he made it so famous that people came to it from all parts of the Greek world. The success of this institution—of a kind quite new at that time—can be explained partly by the personality of its founder, but it was due also to the great variety of disciplines which were taught there from the beginning. These can be divided into two groups. The first, under the general heading of Physics, comprised the natural sciences. One witness, writing about the year 365, included in this group (for example) zoology and botany.[1] The other, under the heading of Mathematics, incorporated arithmetic, geometry, astronomy and harmony. The syllabus of this second group was not new: Plato had taken it from the schools of Magna Graecia set up as a result of Pythagoras' teaching. It was, in particular, that of the philosopher and mathematician Archytas of Tarentum, whom Plato met in 387 or 386, on the occasion of his first visit to Sicily; and it was to survive as the medieval *quadrivium*.

The first work which gives evidence of the founder of the Academy's interest in mathematics is the dialogue called *Meno*, which possibly dates from around 380. (The dates of

---

1. Epicrates, comic poet, fr. 11 (Th. Kock, *Comicorum Atticorum Fragmenta*, Vol. II). See quotation below, p. 37.

the dialogues are for the most part fairly rough approximations.) But the first argument in favour of mathematics as a
framework for academic instruction appears only in the
Republic, which was written between 375 and 370. By 360,
approximately the date of the *Statesman*, it plays a dominant
part in Plato's programme. It held this position until his
death in 347, as is shown by the *Laws*, his last work, which
was left unfinished. Whether this syllabus was actually put
into practice can certainly be called in question, but this
legitimate doubt does not survive the evidence of a critic of
the Academy: the rhetorician Isocrates, who in his *Antidosis*,
written about 355, expresses amazement that so much importance could be accorded to mathematics, and in particular to such difficult disciplines as geometry and astronomy,
but who recognizes that they provide incomparable exercise
for the powers of reasoning.

About the mathematicians whom Plato attracted to or
trained at the Academy we learn principally from a chapter
of the *History of Geometry* written by Aristotle's pupil Eudemus
of Rhodes: the quotation is given below.[1] Adding to this the
evidence of other authors, the following are the likely or
certain facts which the historian can seriously take into
account. Around 375, when he was about forty years old,
the mathematician Theaetetus left the town of Heraclea, on
the Black Sea, to pursue a scientific career in his native city
of Athens. It is not clear whether he settled at the Academy,
but Plato became friendly with him and in 369 dedicated to
his memory the dialogue which bears his name: Theaetetus
had just succumbed to the after-effects of a serious dysentery
contracted in the army. About 370, or perhaps even earlier,
Leodamus of Thasos, in his turn, arrived at the Academy. It
is possible that under the influence of Plato he formulated
as theorems Theaetetus's incomplete discoveries about the
regular solids. A little later, perhaps in 365 or 360, a certain
Leon, whose origins are unknown, compiled an important
handbook of *Elements*, including a general introduction in
which were established—most notably—the criteria for
judging whether a given problem is or is not soluble. Slightly

1. See p. 39.

before 350 there also arrived in Athens the mathematician Eudoxus of Cnidus, who since 362 had been running a school opened by himself at Cyzicus on the east coast of the Sea of Marmara. Eudoxus was neither a pupil of Plato nor a member of the Academy, and he soon left Athens for Cnidus, but he met Plato in Athens and left behind him at the Academy some pupils who had come with him from Cyzicus: Theudius of Magnesia, Athenaeus of Cyzicus, Menaechmus of Proconnesus and his brother Dinostratus. Theudius was the author of a new collection of *Elements*, which must have appeared about the time of Plato's death and which provoked a lively reaction from Speusippus, the new Master of the Academy. For about another ten years, until the death of Speusippus in 339, mathematics took precedence at the Academy. The *Epinomis*, a dialogue published under Plato's name shortly after his death as a sequel to the *Laws*, and which antiquity attributes to his disciple Philip of Opus, reaffirms the founder's doctrine on this point. Thus, reckoning from the opening of the Academy until the death of its second director, we find that the mathematics syllabus inaugurated by Plato was followed in full for a period of forty-six years. The really creative period, however, is much shorter: starting about 375 with the arrival of Theaetetus in Athens and ending with Eudoxus's departure for Cnidus, it is restricted to about twenty-five years.

From what we know of scientific research during this short period, we can say that it saw the working-out of new ideas on which the whole edifice of modern mathematics rests. This working-out, in fact, begins with definitions of the irrational numbers stated by Theaetetus between 375 and 370, and it finished with the *Elements* of Theudius. If before Theaetetus there existed some precise conception of the entities of mathematics and some well-recognized methods of thought, they lacked all axiomatic basis. Plato testifies to this explicitly: Theaetetus's merit lies in his being the first to understand that a mathematical theory develops from definitions which are broad enough to contain within them the solutions of all the problems posed in such a theory.[1] Like-

1. *Theaetetus* 147 D ff. See below p. 66.

wise, even if it is established past dispute that the oldest collection of *Elements* was compiled a good half-century before Theaetetus, by Hippocrates of Chios, and as good as proved that this expounded already, as a series of theorems, the subject-matter of the first four books of Euclid—that is to say, constructions of elementary figures and of certain regular polygons, equalities and similarities of these figures, some problems of division, and problems relating to the circle—it is not before Leon, the second author of *Elements* (in point of time), that the ideas of an axiom, a postulate, an hypothesis—in short, the first principles of mathematics—are acknowledged and defined. Finally, if geometry and arithmetic have arisen as early as the fifth century, the first out of cadastral surveys and the second out of commercial transactions, the initial attempt at a generalization which embraces these specific sciences in its turn, and which can include all mathematics under the same laws, dates only from Eudoxus of Cnidus. It is therefore no exaggeration to give a single generation, comprising Plato's intimates and a few of their rivals, the credit for having inaugurated modern mathematics.

Some texts

Now let us turn to the texts which enlighten us about this development. As we are still dealing with answers to the question 'What is mathematics?' we can leave aside all documentation relating to strictly scientific discoveries. We are concerned here only with the texts which refer to the nature and aim of mathematics.

These texts can be divided into three groups of different age. The earliest group comprises the rare observations on this theme formulated before Plato's time. The oldest goes back to Protagoras, i.e. to a date around 430. It would be useless to search further back in history since Protagoras is the first philosopher to ask himself what is an *art*, a *technē*, in the work which bears the significant title, *On Wrestling and Other Arts*. A second group, represented below only by a selection of quotations, sets out the definitions and classifications of the mathematical sciences accepted by Plato and his contemporaries. We shall note there, on the one hand, the anxiety to dematerialize arithmetic and geometry, so as to make them absolutely distinct from utilitarian computation and geodesy, and on the other, the wish to make mathematics serve philosophy, to which it must reveal the fundamental principles of Being. The third group, also represented only by a selection of opinions, brings together the evidence of the mathematicians who, while insisting like Plato on mathematical abstraction, reacted against the integration of mathematics into philosophy, and made it what it remains today for the greater proportion of mathematicians: a conjecture.

(a) *Predecessors of Plato: the nature of mathematical entities*

Protagoras (*c.* 486–410)

> A circle in fact touches a straight-edge, not at one point only, but in the way that Protagoras, in his refutation of the geometers, said that it did. (Arist. *Metaph.* 998 [a]2)

The geometers against whom Protagoras protested are probably the Pythagorean geometers. Perhaps he was conducting a polemic against Hippocrates of Chios, who (it must be allowed) had either stated explicitly the ideal character of geometric figures, or had implied, at least tacitly, that his science dealt with ideal figures.

Democritus (*c.* 460–370)

> If a cone were cut by a plane parallel to the base, what must we think of the surfaces forming the sections? Are they equal or unequal? For, if they are unequal, they will make the cone irregular as having many indentations, like steps, and unevennesses: but, if they are equal, the sections will be equal, and the cone will appear to have the property of the cylinder and to be made up of equal, not unequal, circles, which is very absurd. (68 B 155)

In analysing this dilemma Democritus rejects both the Pythagorean notion of an ideal figure, and that of a material figure which Protagoras opposed to it. The definition which he put forward described every circular figure as the limit of a polygon, the number of whose sides was increasing to infinity. This definition has not been preserved, but it is presumed in a proof which treats the cone and the cylinder by analogy with the pyramid and the prism. Likewise, we know that Democritus, taking up the problem of tangency again after Protagoras, defined the sphere as 'a sort of angle' c 68 B 155a): he meant by that—using perhaps the very same term as Hippocrates had used in his *Elements*,[1] but with one significant reservation—that every circle forms with its tangent, at the point where they meet, an infinitesimal 'angle' and, separating from it by an equally infinitesimal increase of this angle, ends by closing back on itself. This argument, which puts him (in a sense) half-way between the Pythagoreans and Protagoras, was probably developed in a treatise whose title is revealing: *On the contact of a circle and a sphere.*

Philolaus (second half of fifth century)

> Everything which is known to us has a number, for it is not possible either to perceive or to know anything at all without number. (44 B 4)

We are not certain that this is an authentic quotation. But it nevertheless states fairly exactly a Pythagorean doctrine of which Philolaus was considered the most eminent exponent. According to this theory, every being is a number, or at least the imitation of a number. Far from idealizing the being, Philolaus tended on the contrary to materialize the number, to make it a being in its own right—so making arithmetic, the science of numbers, into a science of real beings. This conception was to reappear, more fully developed and supplemented by a classification of the mathematical sciences, in Archytas, from whom Plato got his inspiration.

Archytas (first half of fourth century)

> The mathematicians seem to me to have arrived at correct conclusions, and it is not therefore surprising that

1. Aristotle, *Analytica priora* 41b 13–22.

they have a true conception of the nature of each individual thing; for, having reached such correct conclusions regarding the nature of the universe, they were bound to see in its true light the nature of particular things as well. Thus they have handed down to us clear knowledge about the speed of the stars, their risings and settings, and about geometry, arithmetic, and sphaeric, and last, not least, about music: for these sciences seem to be sisters, since the two fundamental appearances of the being to which they apply (that is to say number and magnitude) are sisters. (Beginning of the *Harmony*, 47 B 1)

As regards knowledge, the art of arithmetic is far superior to the other arts, in that it deals more clearly with its subject-matter than they do—even geometry. For even where geometry is baffled, arithmetic can complete the proof. And if there is such a thing as a science of the aspects of number, arithmetic contributes to this also. (Taken from *Conversations* 47 B 5)

It can be seen from these two quotations that the mathematicians of Archytas' time claimed for themselves complete responsibility for the central problem of Greek philosophy: the knowledge of real being. Astronomy and harmony—the 'music' of Archytas—are fitted to recognize in natural phenomena the presence of numbers and magnitudes. Sphaeric, the science intermediate between astronomy and geometry, must determine the ideal orbits described by the stars in their motions and define their relationships. Harmony strictly so-called has the same task with regard to the phenomena of sound: it translates them into numbers. Finally geometry and arithmetic, drawing conclusions from sphaeric and harmony respectively, seek the laws which govern them and attempt to define the being which best conforms to these laws. For Archytas, this primordial and perfect being, the origin of all natural things, is the circle, and the numerical relationship which governs it is that of equality, which is the finest 'aspect' of the number. Like Philolaus he thus thinks of the mathematical sciences as physics: as a science whose object is as concrete—though this term no longer holds any meaning for him—as a being can be.

Despite their differences, the opinions assembled in this first group have this much at any rate in common: that if, in practice, pure mathematics is tending to separate itself from applied mathematics, the two disciplines are not nevertheless considered to be intrinsically different. Between the geometry refuted by Protagoras, Protagoras himself, Democritus and Archytas, the only disagreement is over the degree of reality possessed by mathematical entities, not over the fact that they are real. Archytas does not even recognize what we call mathematical abstraction, and unhesitatingly calls ideas such as odd and even, equal and unequal, by the name of 'aspects'. But he is the first man clearly to carry the argument to its ultimate conclusion, and to define 'true reality' in mathematical terms. Because of him, perhaps, and given the influence he apparently had on Plato, a certain ambiguity finds its way into mathematics, which from now on will long be burdened with ontological preoccupations, mixing up knowledge of things themselves with that of the relations between things. This deviation is peculiar to antiquity and has rarely deceived modern mathematicians, apart from those who have wished to believe in the existence of mathematical entities independent of Nature, yet nevertheless real; they have been few. On the other hand, an analogy can easily be established between the conception accepted by Archytas's predecessors —as commonly expressed—and that which prevailed from the Renaissance until the nineteenth century: both grant an objective reality to quantities, magnitudes and forms, assigning to mathematics the task of measuring them and discerning the relationships between them.

(b) Plato and his disciples: ontological mathematics
Meno (c. 380?)

Figure is that in which a solid ends, or figure is the limit (or extremity) of a solid. (76 A)

This definition, the earliest observation about mathematics in Plato's work, has one thing in common with the opinions we have just been analysing: it attributes existence to mathematical objects. But in another respect it differs profoundly from them: it tries to grasp these objects, or at least some of them—in this case, surface—by way of the intellect rather than sight. In fact, what interests Plato here is less the form of the plane figure than its character *qua* plane figure, *qua* surface.

Republic (*c.* 375–370)

Those who are to take part in the highest functions of state must be induced [to apply themselves to the science and study of calculation] not in an amateur spirit, but perseveringly, until, by the aid of pure thought, they come to see the real nature of number. They are to practise calculation, not like merchants or shopkeepers for purposes of buying and selling, but . . . to help in the conversion of the soul itself from the world of becoming to truth and reality. . . . It has a great power of leading the mind upwards and forcing it to reason about pure numbers, refusing to discuss collections of material things which can be seen and touched. (VII 525 B–D *passim*)

Geometers constantly talk of 'operations' like 'squaring', 'applying', 'adding', and so on, as if the object were to *do* something, whereas the true purpose of the whole subject is knowledge—knowledge, moreover, of what eternally exists, not of anything that comes to be this or that at some time and ceases to be. (527 AB)

We ought first to take solid bodies; for the third dimension should come after the second, and that brings us to the cube and all the figures which have depth. (528 B)

Accordingly, we must use the embroidered heaven as a model to illustrate our study of those realities, just as one might use diagrams exquisitely drawn by some consummate artist like Daedalus. An expert in geometry, meeting with such designs, would admire their finished workmanship, but he would think it absurd to study them in all earnest with the expectation of finding in their proportions the exact ratio of any one number to another. (529 DE)

> The students of harmony are just like the astronomers —intent upon the numerical properties embodied in these audible consonances; they do not rise to the level of formulating problems and inquiring which numbers are inherently consonant and which are not, and for what reasons . . . [This undertaking can lead] to the knowledge of beauty and goodness. (531 BC)

The third of these passages commends a discipline which was at that time novel: stereometry, or the study of solids. Plato seeks to introduce this into his classification as the science intermediate between those whose objects are perceptible only by the intellect, viz. arithmetic and plane geometry, and whose those objects are tangible, viz. astronomy and harmony. Stereometry being the science of motionless objects, it appears to him less contingent than these last two. For the hierarchy he establishes here among mathematical sciences corresponds to a hierarchy among the truths propounded by these sciences: perfect truth of the perfect being for arithmetic, the science of number, truth of the second or third degree for the science of solids, or solids in motion.

Philebus (c. 350)

> Taking the technical knowledge employed in handicraft, let us first consider whether one division is more closely concerned with knowledge, and the other less so, so that we are justified in regarding the first kind as the purest, and the second as relatively impure. . . . If, for instance, from any craft you subtract the element of numbering, measuring, and weighing, the remainder will be almost negligible . . . [On the other hand, in the more exact arts] to take first numbering or arithmetic, ought we not to distinguish between that of the ordinary man and that of the philosopher? . . . The ordinary arithmetician, surely, operates with unequal units; his 'two' may be two armies or two cows or two anythings from the smallest thing in the world to the biggest: while the philosopher will have nothing to do with him, unless he consents to make every single instance of his unit precisely equal to every other of its infinite number of

instances. . . . [A similar distinction holds] between the calculating and measurement employed in building or commerce and the geometry and calculation practised in philosophy. (55 D—56 E *passim*)

This extract is no more significant than other similar arguments, which one could take in plenty from dialogues composed after the *Republic*. It has been given preference here for one reason only, that it comes from one of Plato's last works, and thus demonstrates the persistence of his doctrine about the teaching of mathematics in the heart of the Academy. A final quotation, which refers to a famous Lecture on the Supreme Good, delivered by the philosopher shortly before his death, succeeds in locating this teaching within the framework of his metaphysics:

> The majority of those who heard Plato's lecture on the Good saw that they had had a false conception of the subject. They had come with the idea that they would hear about one of the 'goods' recognized as such by men—for example wealth, health, strength and, generally speaking, every exceptional happiness. But when they saw that Plato was discoursing about mathematics, numbers, geometry and astronomy and eventually concluding that the Good is a Unity, they were completely disconcerted. (Aristotle's testimony, as reported by Aristoxenus, *Harm. Elem.* II, p. 30)

Speusippus (*d.* 339)

Among those of Plato's disciples who, following the example of their master, strove to explain Being in mathematical terms, we must mention first his nephew Speusippus, whose ideas on this subject date from the time when Plato was still at the head of the Academy. We shall consider later his theory of numbers (p. 46); for the moment, it is enough to quote Aristotle's account of his crucial doctrine of Being, in one of the numerous passages where he controverts it:

> The mathematician's *number*, which is distinct from all sensible things and the first of all beings, alone has any real existence . . . And so also with magnitudes, surfaces and solids; if one does not reduce Ideas to numbers,

and if one accordingly denies the very existence of Ideas, one will call these objects, as mathematicians themselves do, 'mathematical entities'. (*Metaph.* 1080ᵇ 14)

Xenocrates (394–314)

Some commentators, both ancient and modern, have attributed the doctrine summarized in the above quotation equally to Xenocrates, Speusippus's successor at the head of the Academy. There is plenty of testimony about his analysis of Being in numerical terms. This shows that he arrived, by a slightly different route from Speusippus, at an almost identical conclusion: there would therefore be little use in listing the evidence here. There is, however, one reference to the teaching syllabus of the Academy, which reveals how Plato's pupils interpreted the coincident hierarchies among the mathematical sciences and among beings. Here again, Xenocrates seems very close to the theory put forward in the Lecture on the Supreme Good, but his assertions are more definite than any to be found on this subject, either in Plato's dialogues or in what is left of his Lecture on the Supreme Good.

First we find Ideas and Numbers, which have the same nature, then other beings in succession, namely lines, surfaces, and so on, until we come to the heavenly being and to the sensible beings. (Arist. *Metaph.* 1028ᵇ 24)

Philip of Opus or of Medma (contemporary with the foregoing)

Antiquity credited him with the *Epinomis* (whose title means *Appendix to the Laws*), so making this work a supplement to Plato's *Laws*, which was published after the philosopher's death. Today this attribution is questioned, and several scholars have suggested reassigning the *Epinomis* to Plato. However this may be, it is obviously a work written to spread the doctrine of the Academy at a time when the founder was in his extreme old age, and so provides excellent evidence of the most orthodox Platonist theories. The whole conclusion should really be quoted here, but that would take us out of the way. So let us be content with its first lines, which deal with arithmetic and geometry.

It is essential to learn mathematics, whose primary and most important discipline is the science of numbers, considered in their own right and apart from bodies. The aim of this science is the generation of Odd and Even, and their relation to the nature of other things. Whoever has studied this will tackle next the discipline which is, quite absurdly, called 'geometry', and which is, properly speaking, the science by which numbers not in themselves comparable are made comparable by relating them to the category of surfaces. (990 CD)

Much more than the other members of the Academy, the author of these definitions stresses the fact that mathematics studies relations. Indeed, in recognizing the possibility of falling back on geometrical relations when arithmetical ones fail, and on stereometrical relations when geometrical ones fail, he sees a marvellous principle of continuity. That two irrational square-roots could be compared by way of the square figures whose sides they would form, appears to him an indication of a continuity among beings of different kinds, from the most material to the most ideal. But this interpretation is a personal one, and does not commit the whole Academy. On the other hand, in building up his whole work, which is a vast classification of the sciences, so as to demonstrate that mathematics is the key to all understanding, and particularly to that supreme understanding which is the philosopher's goal, he places himself at the centre of Plato's teaching.

Let us assess the views collected in this second section. Whether we consider Plato or his immediate disciples, the status given to mathematics in the doctrine which governs the tradition of the Academy emerges quite clearly from their unanimous evidence: it is the science *par excellence*, that which Plato calls simply *epistēmē*, and that which leads—as much by its method as by its proper object—to a knowledge of True Being. Before the Master became convinced that the fundamental type of being, i.e. the Idea, is nothing but a number, he did (it is true) still place dialectic above arithmetic. But the invention of this novel discipline, which he never regarded as essentially different or distinct from mathematics, did not in any way detract from the triumphs of understanding represented successively by astronomy, stereometry, plane geometry and the science of numbers: dialectic is merely the top rung of this ladder. Once the identity of the Idea with Number was established, however, traditional mathematics was considered to suffice by itself.

This practice of treating mathematics as concerned with a knowledge of Being has led some historians of science to use the phrase *ontological mathematics*. In this respect Plato is manifestly continuing the work of Archytas, which was itself a development out of Pythagoreanism. On one very important point, however, Plato broke line. In defining Being as a number, or as the imitation of a number, the Pythagoreans (as already explained) treated numbers as material things. This conception of numbers, which seems extraordinary to us nowadays, took in their arithmetic the concrete form of representing numbers by points grouped in squares or rectangles. It may even have been the habit of calculating with numbers depicted in this way that led them gradually to the idea of numbers as material. Plato, on the contrary, refused to regard either ideas or numbers as material objects. For him they are intelligible objects, realities inaccessible to the senses. Had he given these objects a place within the human intellect, he would then—2,300 years before the author of the Bourbaki definition quoted at the beginning of this chapter—have initiated a remarkably similar train of thought. For, like him, he already accepts the ambiguous idea of 'abstract forms', and if he has not yet recognized that these forms are in part a creation of the mind, he is none the less lifelike an example of the mathematician as Bourbaki conceives him; since, in fact, he was constantly projecting onto the universe and onto reality the mathematical structures populating his thoughts. So, however different the development of his conception of mathematical objects may have been from the origin of the Bourbaki definition, a common experience unites them— namely, the profound sense of an ideal mathematical universe.

(c) Mathematicians contemporary with Plato: axiomatic mathematics

Eudoxus of Cnidus (390–337)
His conception of mathematics has not come down to us in
the form of particular reflexions or definitions. Antiquity
quotes his definition of Number, and the most one can say
about it is that it is devoid of any ontological tendency.

Number is a determinate multitude. (Fr D. 66)

There is more to be deduced from his general theory of
proportions, but this cannot be dealt with here, and we need
only refer the reader to the chapter devoted to this subject
(p. 89).

Menaechmus (who wrote between 360 and 340)
Three important extracts survive from an argument
about the principles of mathematics in which he is ranged
against Speusippus.

Some, like Speusippus and Amphinomus, thought
proper to call all propositions *theorems*, regarding the
name of theorems as more appropriate than that of
problems to theoretic sciences, especially as these deal
with eternal objects. For there is no becoming in things
eternal, so that neither could the problem have any
place with them, since it promises the generation and
making of what has not before existed, e.g. the construction of an equilateral triangle, or the describing of
a square on a given straight line, or the placing of a
straight line at a given point. Hence they say it is better
to assert that all propositions are of the same kind, and
that we regard the generation that takes place in them
as referring not to actual *making* but to *knowledge*, when
we treat things existing eternally as if they were subject
to becoming; in other words, we may say that everything is treated by way of theorem and not by way of
problem.
Others on the contrary, like the mathematicians of
the school of Menaechmus, thought it right to call them
all problems, describing their purpose as twofold,
namely in some cases to furnish the thing sought, in
others to take a determinate object and see either what

it is, or of what **nature**, or what is its property, or in what relations it stands to something else. (Proclus, *Comm. in Eucl. lib. I*, p. 77)

The three propositions advanced by supporters of the idea of 'theorems' appear again, in almost identical terms, in Euclid. In the first book of *Elements* they figure as propositions No. 1, 2 and 46 respectively. But Amphinomus, Speusippus and Menaechmus lived well before Euclid, and the *Elements* from which they took their examples were either those written by Theudius or the even earlier set by Leon. So their controversy confirms that these *Elements* used sometimes one, sometimes the other of the two terms in question. It proves equally that thought about these two terms goes back at least to the author of the *Elements* used. Now, even though the argument might appear rather futile to someone who is more interested in the content of the theorems than in the philosophical meaning of a geometric truth, it is quite a different matter for a mathematician who, in the very heart of Plato's Academy, denies to certain of these truths an eternal existence, or rather any existence independent of the geometer's own discovery. And if the word *problem*, borrowed from educational practice, has little meaning in philosophy, the word *theorem* on the contrary is indissolubly linked (by the verb from which it is derived, *theorein*) to the idea of *contemplation*, and thus to the whole Platonic doctrine of knowledge, whose goal is the contemplation of pure Ideas.

Again, the term *element* is used in two senses, as Menaechmus says. For that which is the means of obtaining is an element of that which is obtained. In this sense many things may even be said to be elements of each other, for they are obtained from one another. Thus from the fact that the exterior angles of rectilineal figures are together equal to four right angles we deduce the number of right angles equal to the internal angles taken together, and *vice versa*. Such an element is like a *lemma*. But the term *element* is otherwise used of that into which, being more simple, the composite is divided: and in this sense we can no longer say that everything is an element of everything, but only that things which are more of the nature of principles are elements of those which stand to them in the relation of results, as postulates are elements of theorems. (Proclus, ibid; p.72)

The word *lemma* also comes from the *Elements* of Theudius or Leon. It indicates the proposition *taken*—*lemma* is derived etymologically from *to take*—by the mathematician as the subject of a demonstration. Thus all Euclid's propositions are commonly called *lemmas*. As regards the place of the term *element* in the handbook of geometry to which Menaechmus refers, it seems probable that it did not by itself provide an adequate basis for discussion. Admittedly, this word appeared only in the title of the handbook, and Menaechmus's comment is an attempt to explain the title in terms of the content of the work. Originally, in conformity to its etymological sense, the word *element* seems to have meant simply one unit in a rank, or a file. The first mathematicians who applied it to a collection of theorems were, accordingly, well aware of the fact that the theorems followed one another, in sequence, like soldiers in a parade, or the letters in an ABC.

> Some claim that all these things (i.e. the first principles) are alike *postulates*, in the same way as they maintain that all things that are sought are problems. . . . Others call them all *axioms* in the same way as they regard as theorems everything that requires demonstration. (Proclus, ibid., p. 181)

The reference to the controversy about theorems and problems shows that Menaechmus's conception of geometry based it entirely on *postulates*, while Speusippus supported a geometry whose first principles would have all been called *axioms*. Evidently, the *Elements* of Theudius or Leon were already using these two terms with the meanings they were to preserve in Euclid, and in modern textbooks.

What is the meaning of all this, and in what respect does it herald the advent of a conception of mathematics quite different from Plato's? In opting for postulates rather than axioms, Menaechmus was reducing mathematics to an exercise in logic, which would consist in developing all the consequences of certain initial premises which were accepted only by a sort of convention, and recognized as hypothetical. In this way, he broke completely with the Platonic idea of perfect beings underlying the expressions of mathematics. As for Speusippus, compelled to admit that the fundamental truths of mathematics could not all be identified with 'beings', in the Platonic sense, he seems to have retired to a second line of defence, from which he regarded as beings the certitudes resulting from a common agreement on fundamental ideas, that is to say, the axioms. Aristotle elsewhere confirms that he abandoned the theory of ideas, but that he still believed in mathematical entities, or at least in mathematical essences. In opting for 'theorems', in preference to 'problems', he defined mathematics—still in a Platonic sense—as the contemplation of these essences. In choosing 'axioms' rather than 'postulates', he affirmed that the relations between these essences spring, not from hypotheses, but from laws which are in some sense inherent in the universe, and expressed in the first principles of mathematical treatises. That two objects both equal to a third object are equal to one another—the first axiom of Euclidean geometry —must have seemed to him not merely an objective truth, but an actual expression of the world of essences, while Menaechmus could see in it only a hypothesis of the human mind.

Both men, however, in keeping with their own conception of mathematics, favoured a more moderate doctrine which separated first principles into axioms and postulates. This doctrine can be traced back to the *Elements* of Theudius or Leon, and introduced all the ideas and terminology which we find again in Euclid. Without laying so much emphasis on the meaning of the words as Speusippus and Menaechmus did later, this doctrine had, nevertheless, consciously abandoned the ontological mathematics of Platonism and produced what we call *axiomatic mathematics*—a name which, despite Speusippus's interpretation, definitively underlines the subjective character of the first principles. Simultaneously, the originators of this revolutionary conception disclaimed all analysis of the nature and presuppositions of these principles, so as to concentrate all their efforts on to developing their logical consequences—a field which ontological mathematics, concentrating rather on the analysis of the principles, left undeveloped. The direction thus taken is the same as that which Bertrand Russell's definition (quoted at the beginning of this chapter) allotted to mathematical research. Its effect in ancient times was to give a new vigour to those sciences which had been weakened by the analytical dissections of the later Pythagoreans and of Plato's most faithful disciples, and to prepare the ground for the erection, rather later, of the three most amazing monuments of mathematical genius in antiquity: Euclid's *Elements*, Archimedes' treatises on surfaces bounded by curves of the second degree, and Apollonius of Perga's *Conics*.

Mathematics and physics

Having ceased to concern itself with external reality, pure mathematics was forced to exclude the physical sciences from its immediate scope, even those sciences, such as harmony and astronomy, whose structure was then accepted as mathematical. Still on this point: although in antiquity the problem was not put in exactly the same terms, ancient mathematicians had to face the same difficulties as their modern successors. This result was emphasized above all by Aristotle, whose philosophical and scientific position was formed at the Academy, where he remained for twenty years after his entry in 367 B.C. The views he reports on this subject can be taken as those of the mathematicians with whom he was in regular touch up till the death of Plato in 347: in general he made them his own, and he uses them to express his own views. Numerous texts could be quoted, notably from the oldest parts of the *Metaphysics*, but it is enough to quote here the most complete and explicit, which undoubtedly dates from before 341.

> We have now to consider whether it belongs to one science or to different sciences to inquire into what mathematicians call axioms and into substances. It is manifest that the inquiry into these axioms belongs to

one science and that the science of the philosopher; for they hold good for all existing things, and not for some one genus in particular to the exclusion of others. Everyone makes use of them because they belong to being *qua* being, and each genus is part of being. Men use them, however, just so far as is sufficient for their purpose, that is, so far as the genus, to which the demonstrations they offer have reference, extends. Since then it is clear that they hold good for all things *qua* being (for this is what they have in common), the person who knows about being *qua* being must investigate these axioms too. This is why none of those who study the special sciences tries to enunciate anything about them, their truth or falsehood: neither the geometer, for instance, nor the mathematician does so, though it is true that some of the physicists have made the attempt, and not unnaturally, seeing that they supposed that the inquiry into the whole of nature and into being belonged to them alone. But since there is a class of inquirer above the physicists (nature being only one particular genus of being) it is for the thinker whose inquiry is universal and who investigates primary substance to inquire into these axioms as well. (*Metaph.* 1005ᵃ 19)

This passage shows how decisive a break the mathematicians' abandonment of ontological speculations had provoked between the mathematical and physical sciences. It is so clear that it requires no comment. The mathematicians' radically negative attitude towards physics, however, in no way called in question the existence of mathematical structures, not only in the natural sciences but also among the objects and natural phenomena which were their province. They required only that the truly physical part of any science be carefully distinguished from the truly mathematical part. According to Aristotle, who is still our best source of information here, they allotted to physics the reasoned observation of facts, to mathematics the explanation of causes, but they did not permit themselves to trace causes back to external reality.

But there is another way in which the cause may differ

from the fact: the investigation of the two things may belong to different sciences. This is the case where the subjects are so related that one falls under the other, in the way that optics is related to geometry, mechanics to stereometry, harmonics to arithmetic, and phenomena to astronomy. Some of these sciences are in practice called by the same name, e.g. mathematical and nautical astronomy, mathematical and acoustical harmonics. Here knowledge of the fact is the business of sense-perception, that of the cause is the business of mathematicians. . . . Mathematics is concerned with forms; mathematical properties are not predicated of any substratum; for even though geometrical facts are predicated of some substratum, they are not predicated of it *as such*. (*Analyt. post.* 78^b 35)

Thus if physics, in the ancient sense of the word—that is to say, the science of the nature of Being—is no longer for Aristotle a mathematical science, as it had been earlier for Plato, in all the principal disciplines bequeathed to modern physics (optics, acoustics and mechanics) the mathematicians of the Academy were already supporting the view which prevailed among physicists in the nineteenth century. Like their modern successors, indeed, the contemporaries of the young Aristotle allowed that, in principle, the observed facts must depend on a set of relations whose validity was a matter of mathematics. They were so firmly convinced on this point that they even demanded that mathematical explanation should prevail *a priori* over the apparent contradictions of observation. We know, for example, that in astronomy the philosopher Heraclides of Pontus, a pupil of Plato's from 365, wanted to subordinate everything to the following rule:

What circular, uniform and regular movements must be assumed in order to account for the phenomena?

This way of stating the problem, accepted even by an astronomer of Eudoxus' standing, illustrated perfectly the part which mathematics was called upon to play *vis-à-vis* experience.

Faith in the possibility of explaining natural phenomena mathematically dated from before Plato's time. It is characteristic of antiquity. In Plato's era, however, in spite of the cautious attitudes of the greatest mathematicians, it encountered some opposition, whose existence itself proves that scientific criticism had not failed to probe even the most sacred principles of physics. The best evidence on this subject concerns harmony, and although it comes from a treatise written by Aristoxenus after 322, it refers once more to discussions begun by the first generation of Plato's pupils.

Of our answers we endeavour to supply proofs that will be in agreement with the phenomena, in this unlike our predecessors. For some of these introduced extraneous reasoning and, rejecting the senses as inaccurate, fabricated mental principles, asserting that height and depth of pitch consist in certain numerical ratios and relative rates of vibration, a theory utterly extraneous to the subject and quite at variance with the phenomena. While others, dispensing with reason and demonstration, confined themselves to isolated dogmatic statements, not being successful either in enumeration of the mere phenomena. (*Harm. Elem.* II, p. 32)

Curricula and syllabuses

We are apt to think of the Academy as depicted in the famous fresco by Raphael in the Stanza della Segnatura, at the Vatican: as he passes by small groups of disciples who are poring over various pieces of work, Plato gives them here some work for the day, there a piece of advice, while a number of older men are gravely handling geometrical instruments, or pondering over the treatises which they are writing. This vision is not far from the truth. At most it should be added that these groups of people did not normally collect in the vast halls of a Renaissance palace, but under the colonnades of the porticos surrounding the gymnasium at the Academy, and that their discussions were led by other masters when Plato was busy elsewhere. Here, for example, is how the comic poet Epicrates described (about

365) the activity of a natural history class clustered round Speusippus:

> They were discussing nature. They were trying to establish definitions by first distinguishing from each other the animal kingdom, species of trees and families of vegetables. They tried to find out to what category the pumpkin belongs. To begin with they said nothing, bending their heads to help them think. Then suddenly, while the others, exhausted, were still searching, one of them said; 'It is a vegetable of spherical shape.' Then another: 'It is a herb.' Then yet another: 'It is a tree.' But Plato, who came up at this moment, asked them without getting angry, very gently in fact, to go back to the beginning of the definition of the pumpkin, starting by saying to what fundamental category it belongs. So they went back to their distinctions. (Fr. 11)

In the case of mathematics, the teaching must have been very much as described in a pleasant episode of Plato's *Meno*. The following problem is to be solved: how many feet long will the side of a square be, whose area is double that of a two-foot square? The master begins by repeating to the pupil, with the help of a sketch, the definition of a square, some of its properties, what is meant by doubling an area, etc. Then he makes him calculate in turn the areas of the two squares. The pupil, having then hastily decided that, in view of the areas being double one another, the sides must also be double one another, suggests a side four feet long; then, after being corrected, the mathematical average between two feet and four feet, viz. three feet. The master points out his mistake to him and from then on, without asking him to do any more than grasp the stages of his proof point by point, he leads him to the correct solution.

The *Republic* and the *Laws* show us in detail how the programme of studies was organized. It begins with a series of preparatory studies which the pupils have to pursue between their seventh and seventeenth or eighteenth years; but this course is outside the Academy, which only takes older students. It is devoted to practical exercises, preparing the adolescent to administer his possessions and to serve in the army, and at the same time training his powers of reasoning: arithmetic, the geometry of lengths and areas, calendrical astronomy.

After this course come three years of military service, which delay the start of the academic studies proper until the age of twenty or twenty-one. The pupil who is felt, during the first course, to be capable of moving on to higher studies then enters the Academy, or at least the ideal institution which Plato hopes for in his model republic. The course on which he now embarks extends in principle over fifteen years, of which the first ten are devoted to mathematics and the rest to dialectic. Speusippus, Xenocrates, Aristotle and most of the philosophers coming from the Academy certainly followed this syllabus from beginning to end, but many other pupils were satisfied with shorter periods. As a general rule, they studied several different disciplines simultaneously.

> They will be offered all at one time the sciences which they have studied at random in their adolescence, so that they can get a broader view of the relationships between these sciences and by this means become acquainted with the true nature of reality. (*Repub.* 537 C)

We can see that Plato did not follow in this practical programme the intellectual direction of philosophical inquiry, by which the mind must rise in succession from the more concrete to the more abstract sciences, in order finally to grasp the nature of Being. Such inquiry was—admittedly —reserved for the years of Dialectic, during which the knowledge gained from the study of mathematics was recapitulated. On the other hand, he did stress the need to compare different disciplines, so as to bring to light their common elements and guide the student towards generalizations. The programme of mathematical inquiry opens with this exercise, by which Plato also indicates its goal.

We are familiar with the results obtained by mathematicians trained at or stimulated by the Academy, thanks to the chapter in the *History of Geometry* by Eudemus of Rhodes from which were taken most of the historical and biographical information assembled above (under the heading 'Historical Data' p. 15). These results conform very well to the direction given by Plato to mathematical research, while reflecting also to some extent the natural development of the science. An impartial historian would say that by the beginning of the fourth century, mathematics had reached a point at which a revision of the basic data and the development of more general views had become necessary. The discoveries of Eudoxus, which owed nothing to Plato's influence, prove that the need for generalization was not, in fact, peculiar to the Academy. But Eudemus, who writes about 320, is one of Plato's admirers, and his natural propensity to simplify history leads him to credit the Academy alone with developments which are easily recognized in the mathematical treatises of the preceding generation.

The two summaries of his introductory chapter which have come down to us are noticeably dominated by this argument. The first in particular demands our attention because it shows how Eudemus tried to ascribe to the influence of Plato—no doubt on the basis of good historical evidence—works of which Eudoxus was the initiator.

> In mathematics at that time great advances were made, for which Plato was certainly responsible. For he put the problems to which mathematicians set about finding solutions. The study of commensurability then reached the *height of its development* [text uncertain] for the first time, and likewise the problems of *numbers* [text uncertain], Eudoxus's pupils having refashioned the *traditional ancient arithmetic* [text uncertain]. Geometry also made considerable progress. This in fact was the birth of analytical method and *diorismi*. (*Index Academicus*, p. 16)

The second summary, much better known and much more complete, tends to obscure the leading idea in a mass of information, but Eudemus' intention is evident if one reads it in the light of the first.

Plato caused mathematics in general and geometry in

39

particular to make a very great advance, owing to his own zeal for these studies: for every one knows that he even filled his writings with mathematical discourses and strove on every occasion to arouse enthusiasm for mathematics in those who took up philosophy. At this time too lived Leodamas of Thasos, Archytas of Taras, and Theaetetus of Athens, by whom the number of theorems was increased and a further advance was made towards a more scientific grouping of them.

Younger than Leodamas were Neoclides and his pupil Leon, who added many things to what was known before their time, so that Leon was actually able to make a collection of the elements more carefully designed in respect both of the number of propositions proved and of their utility, besides which he invented *diorismi*, the object of which is to determine when the problem under investigation is possible of solution and when impossible.

Eudoxus of Cnidus, a little younger than Leon, who had been associated with the pupils of Plato, was the first to increase the number of the so-called general theorems: he also added three other mean proportionals to the three already known, and multiplied the theorems which originated with Plato about the section, applying to them the method of analysis.

Amyclas of Heraclea, one of the pupils of Plato, Menaechmus, a pupil of Eudoxus who had also studied with Plato, and Dinostratus, his brother, made the whole of geometry still more perfect. Theudius of Magnesia had the reputation of excelling in mathematics as well as in the other branches of philosophy: for he put together the elements admirably and made many partial theorems more general. Again Athenaeus of Cyzicus, who lived about the same time, became famous in other branches of mathematics and most of all in geometry. These men consorted together in the Academy and conducted their investigations in common.

Hermotimus of Colophon carried further the investigations already opened up by Eudoxus and Theaetetus, discovered many propositions of the *Elements* and compiled some portion of the theory of loci. Philip .of Medma, who was a pupil of Plato and took up mathematics at his instance, not only carried out his investigations in accordance with Plato's instructions but also set himself to do whatever in his view contributed to the philosophy of Plato. (Proclus, *Comm. in Eucl. lib. I*, p. 66)

Such is the enthusiastic evidence of a philosopher who could still read for himself almost all the works of the authors he mentions, and who with their help could trace the broad outlines of this period of the history of science. We can close our chapter with this idyllic view of the Academy, in many ways so close to that immortalized by Raphael. But it is the historian's duty to point out that this represents no more than part of the truth about the years before Plato's death. For while—undeniably—philosophy was highly regarded in mathematics, and mathematics itself found in philosophy the justification of its own line of research, ten years later, in a programme vaster than the founder of the Academy had advocated, specialization had prevailed over integration. And around 340 B.C. the grating voice of the aged Isocrates echoed the murmur of the sceptics who, while admitting the great progress within mathematics, remarked that this had in no way increased the philosophers' ability to run their own affairs, as Plato had dreamed it would:

I recommend those who are embarking on the study of geometry and astronomy to devote all their energy and intelligence to them. For I declare that, even if these disciplines cannot make better men of them, they have at least the advantage of keeping young people out of mischief: and I am convinced that no more useful or more suitable activity than these could be found for them. But at a later age, after the examinations which qualify one for the rights of an adult, I maintain that these activities are less appropriate. I would, in fact, say that some of those who have carried the study of these disciplines to the point of teaching them in their turn do not know how to put to proper use the sciences they possess and prove in all circumstances of life to be less judicious than their pupils and even—though I hardly dare suggest it—than their own servants. (*Panathen.* 27–28)

How much truth is there in this disillusioning statement from one of Plato's former rivals? Not very much, to be sure, but this at least, that the teachers of mathematics then active at the Academy set themselves up to be specialists, instead of distinguishing themselves as models of philosophical wisdom. As Isocrates insists, this is less a failure of mathematics than a failure of Plato's declared ambition to base wisdom on mathematics. A historian must draw the same conclusion as he, but, remarking in addition that this failure coincides with a trend towards specialization which developed in particular after Plato's death, he must in all justice admit that this conclusion holds good only for an Academy in which the enlivening influence of the founder was no longer felt. For, if Plato's programme did not fully survive the thinker who had animated it throughout his life, his temporary success is shown by the pupils whom he himself trained in philosophy by way of mathematical modes of thought—notably, the greatest of all, Aristotle. And it is the historian's duty not to forget this fact.

II

Arithmetic

Antiquity speaks ambiguously about the country in which the science of arithmetic was born. Pythagoras is generally given the credit for having introduced the subject to the Greeks, but he is sometimes shown as having learned it in Egypt, at others in Phoenicia. Aristoxenus supported the first hypothesis, Eudemus seems to have tended rather towards the second. In writing their respective histories of the subject, they agreed at least that—whatever its native country—it was practised there only for purposes of commerce, whilst the Greeks transformed it into a theoretical study. Historically speaking, however, their evidence is valueless: this is no more than the speculations of philosophers developing a theme already dear to Plato. Inadvertently, however, they inform us what philosophy expected of arithmetic at the time they were writing—or rather, what it had expected of it in the generation before their own, at the time when the Science of Number was being worked out. Therein lies the real interest of their statements.

According to Aristoxenus, arithmetic would, in the hands of Pythagoras, have become the science which led on to the knowledge of things:

> For Pythagoras compared everything to numbers, Number possessing everything and all numbers being logically related to one another. (*On Arithmetic*, Fr. 23)

Obscure at first glance, this statement is clarified when one

43

considers it from the point of view of that 'ontological mathematics' which was familiar to the contemporaries of Archytas and Plato. Aristoxenus himself explains the least intelligible element in it, the idea of things being *possessed* by numbers, using the following example:

> The crises and turns of diseases seem to occur on odd days, because uneven numbers *possess* a beginning, a middle and an end, just as crises have an initial phase, an acute phase and a declining phase. (Ibid.)

According to Eudemus, in its final stage of development arithmetic would become 'exact knowledge of numbers' (Fr. 133), after having passed successively through the stages of 'sensible perception' and 'reasoned calculus'. So his opinion agrees with that of Aristoxenus, in so far as he treats 'knowledge of numbers' as belonging to the final stage of research in arithmetic.

Principles of the theory of numbers: Speusippus

Before examining the meaning of the formula 'knowing numbers', let us quickly take stock of the treatises devoted to this subject. Although these have left few traces, they were numerous, particularly in the scientific output of the Academy. From the generation before Plato, there remains in the list of Democritus's writings a single title, *Numbers*, and from Archytas the thoughts on the aim of mathematics quoted above (p. 20). From the Academy itself there survive chiefly bare titles: two treatises by Xenocrates were entitled *On Numbers* and *Theory of Numbers*; likewise two treatises by Philip of Opus were called *Arithmetica* and *On Polygonal Numbers*; then there was a study of a related branch of arithmetic, the *Means*, and finally the treatise by Speusippus *On the Pythagorean Numbers*, of which one large fragment is still extant. It should be added that, up to the period of Plato's death, arithmetic—despite its new name—was also known by its older name of *logistics*, which took into account merely its origin as a computative science. Archytas did not know it by any other name, Plato often still referred to it in this way, and Xenocrates was to give an eight-volume work the title *Logistica*. Thus the neologism in use in certain Pythagorean circles from about the time that Plato was writing the *Gorgias* (*c*. 390 B.C.) did not easily supersede the name established as a result of current scholastic practice.

We should like to know which of the above works succeeded in playing, up to the time of Euclid, the part taken in geometry by the *Elements* of Leon or Theudius: namely that of collecting together in a useful and complete handbook the successive discoveries of the most important arithmeticians. As we shall see later, the treatise of Speusippus is presented as a synthesis of previous work on various aspects of numbers, and even its title seems to underline this historical intention. But there is nothing to indicate that it claimed to provide posterity with the classic exposition of arithmetic. At best, Speusippus's apparent anxiety to get it accepted as authentically Pythagorean would tend to prove that, when he was putting out his own work, no authoritative manual yet existed. One wonders also whether the *Elements* of Leon or Theudius already included, as Euclid's did later, books devoted to theorems in arithmetic. However this may be, the subject-matter of this hypothetical handbook can be found in books VII, VIII and IX of Euclid's *Elements*, as well as in some later works which mixed ancient knowledge with more recent developments. As a general rule, one should accept as genuinely ancient only those chapters to which some piece of evidence dating from the fourth century happens to allude, and mistrust all late references. There are in fact, few fields in which writers have been less scrupulous in claiming the authority of their illustrious forerunners. But the most reliable data place the three aforementioned books of Euclid in the historical period which here concerns us. Our documentary basis, though incomplete, is accordingly broad and solid.

Let us go back to the principles of the theory of numbers. Whereas modern arithmetic has developed above all the art of computation, and has explored by algebraical means the theory of relations between numbers, ancient arithmeticians set out to 'know numbers'. What did they mean by that?

The most direct reply to this question is that implicit in the different definitions of Number formulated by Plato's contemporaries. While they were all unsure about the notion of quantity, they were remarkably unanimous on one point: number is composed of units. Eudoxus alone is an exception, conceiving of number as a 'determinate multitude', on account of his own much higher and more general idea of arithmetic. Let us be content with the compromise definition adopted by Euclid:

A number is a multitude composed of units. (*Elem.* VII, Def. 2)

The mathematicians' fondness for the word 'unit' springs from the fact that they were in the habit of picturing numbers, concretely, as figures composed of points or (if one likes) as quantities of points arranged in a figure. According to tradition, this conception dated back to Thales, and even as far as the Egyptians. It is certainly of very great antiquity, but it is not seriously attested before the Pythagorean Petron of Himera, who lived in the first half of the fifth century. 'Knowing numbers' therefore involved being familiar, not only with these figures, but also with their properties, just as in geometry one must know not only the triangle or the square but also the properties which characterize them. Sometimes, the points were merely arranged along a straight line, sometimes they were formed into squares or rectangles, the points then being set out not on the sides of the figure but throughout its area, at its corners, and at the intersections of the imaginary straight lines which divided the figure into squares. Thus the numbers 2 and 3 were represented by lines of two and three points, while the number 9, for example, could take the form either of a square field with sides of three points, or of a line of nine points. In more complex combinations, triangles and regular polygons were also used.

Starting from this conception—or rather from this image —of Number, mathematicians were led to take a special interest in numbers capable of forming regular figures: squares, cubes, etc. This is the right place to quote the summary of Speusippus's treatise *On the Pythagorean Numbers* preserved by Iamblichus, a neo-Platonist of the third to fourth century A.D.

> Up to the middle of his work, Speusippus deals admirably with linear numbers, then with polygonal numbers and various plane numbers, as well as with solid numbers. He then studies the five figures which give their shapes to the elements of the universe, along with their respective properties and their common characteristics, their analogies and mutual relations. (Fr. 4)

At first sight the programme which Speusippus followed lacks unity. What are the theorems on the five regular polyhedra to do, *after* the chapters devoted to numbers? In actual fact it is these theorems which explain all the rest. According to a theory developed in Plato's *Timaeus*, the five polyhedra should correspond mathematically to the five elements of which all things are composed. But they, in their turn, are composed of simpler mathematical elements: namely, surfaces and lines. So this picture of a thing itself reduces to simpler ontological principles. Conversely, by making these principles one's starting point and showing how a line generates a surface, a surface a solid, and a solid a physical element, one can explain the whole of creation in terms of mathematical figures. Now Speusippus had no intention of doing anything else, but instead of going by way of figures, conducting his demonstration geometrically and stereometrically, he goes by way of numbers, and proceeds arithmetically. He was thus able to reduce all Nature to numbers, and these numbers to certain initial numbers expressing such principles as odd and even, the one and the many, the divisible and the indivisible, etc. The first part of his work thus studies linear, plane and solid numbers, and the way they are generated, then deals at length with the five numbers considered to be equivalent to the five regular polyhedra. The second part, from which an important extract will be quoted later in this chapter (p. 57), returns to the initial numbers, and analyses them in the hope of discovering the principles shared by numbers and things.

Evidently Speusippus remained faithful to ontological mathematics: after Plato's death, indeed—his treatise dates from after this event—he was more than a late representative of this point of view. But he reveals to us, at the same time, the technical programme of the theory of numbers, as its initiators had drawn it up: this is here his greatest value to us. As to the period to which the actual content of his arithmetic refers, this is determined more or less by his claims to have drawn his knowledge from a mysterious treatise by the Pythagorean Philolaus of Croton. Philolaus had lived in the second half of the fifth century, but only in the years 390 to 370 does one find a real interest being taken in what was then supposed to have been his teaching: namely, the explanation of Nature in terms of Numbers. Plato alludes to this doctrine for the first time in the *Phaedo*, written about 385: the mathematicians used by Speusippus may have published their works during the same period.

Linear numbers. Proportion

The first chapter of Speusippus's programme covers linear numbers. Once one has divided these into odd and even, the only ones of serious interest are the prime numbers. They are, in fact, the only ones which cannot be displayed except by a line, whence the name 'rectilinear numbers' invented for them by the Pythagorean Thymaridas of Paros, who was probably one of Speusippus's informants. All the non-prime numbers, on the other hand, can be displayed by a rectangular surface. On this distinction hinges a first analysis of numbers, aimed at establishing the ideas of 'common factor' and of numbers 'prime to one another'. Then, this analysis having given rise to the conception of the 'ratio' between two numbers, a new analysis established the definition of this term. Finally, a recognition of the relationships between these ratios leads on to the theory of proportion.

The whole of this development was carried over into Book

VII of Euclid's *Elements*, of which it makes up the first part. His first theorem, which remained the foundation of all reflection about proportionate quantities right up to the time of Eudoxus's general theory of proportions, has the following effect:

> Two unequal numbers being set out, and the less being continually subtracted in turn from the greater, if the number which is left never measures the one before it until a unit is left, the original numbers will be prime to one another. (*Elem.* VII, Prop. 1)

The method of calculation established by this theorem is applicable only to numbers. That is why, for a long time, it was not possible to disentangle from it a general theory of the relations between any two mathematical objects of whatever kind. This procedure was known in antiquity by the name of *antanairesis* or *anthyphairesis*, which can be translated as 'reciprocal subtraction'.

After this theorem, Euclid shows first how two or more numbers which are not prime to one another are bound to have a highest common factor. Then he bases on the idea of a factor, which he likens to a unit of measurement and considers as a part of the number, the idea of a ratio or fraction —without, however, using either of these two terms, or envisaging fractions having the numerator greater than the denominator.

> Any number is either a part or parts of any number, the less of the greater. (*Elem.* VII, Prop. 4)

In other words, every number is either a factor of another larger number, or contains a finite number of factors in common with it: these factors, or parts, being unity when the given numbers are prime to one another. Thus, 4 is part of 8; 6 contains 3 parts of 8, each equal to 2; 5 is made up of 5 parts of 8, each equal to unity. Moreover, if other numbers, when compared with one another in the same way, prove to be parts one of another in the same ratio as the first two numbers compared, if it turns out (e.g.) that 5 is part of 10 in the same ratio as 4 is part of 8—which is called 'being the same part'—a recognition of the equality of the two ratios soon gives rise to the distinct notion of 'proportion'. Nevertheless, this notion remained linked to the narrow conception of numbers which are 'the same part' (or 'the same parts') of other numbers. And this conception was in its turn linked to the idea that, in order to be 'the same part', one must have 'the same *antanairesis*'—that is to say, that both the number of reciprocal subtractions practised on the two pairs of numbers being compared, and the order of these subtractions, must be the same.

Several theorems serve to show how the equality of two ratios is preserved when their numerators and denominators respectively are added together, or subtracted from each other:

$$\text{if } \frac{a}{b} = \frac{c}{d} \text{ , it follows that } \frac{a}{b} = \frac{a+c}{b+d} \text{ and similarly } \frac{a-c}{b-d}$$

But the climax of this first theory of 'the same part' is the theorem relating to the exchange of terms of proportion $\left(\text{if } \frac{a}{b} = \frac{c}{d} \text{ , it follows that } \frac{a}{c} = \frac{b}{d}\right)$:

> If a number be a part of a number, and another be the same part of another, alternately also, whatever part or parts the first is of the third, the same part, or the same parts, will the second also be of the fourth. (*Elem.* VII, Prop. 9)

The demonstration deals for a start with the special case in which the denominator is a multiple of the numerator. In this case, in fact, the relationship of the numerator to the denominator is of the kind already dealt with—namely, a proportion in which one ratio is obtained from a second by adding to its numerator and denominator numbers proportional respectively to this numerator and denominator. Now two terms resulting from such an addition have been proved to be proportional to the parts added to these two terms. It follows that the denominators concerned are proportional to their numerators, which is what we set out to prove.

For example, in the proportion $\frac{a}{b}=\frac{c}{d}$, let us assume that the denominator is three times the numerator; this proportion can then be expressed as follows:

$$\frac{a}{a+2a}=\frac{c}{c+2c}$$

But, according to the above theorem,

$$\frac{a+2a}{c+2c}=\frac{a}{c}$$

In this case, however, it is conceded that $a+2a=b$

and that $c+2c=d$

Therefore $\frac{a}{c}=\frac{b}{d}$

Q.E.D.

Plane numbers and solid numbers

The second chapter of Speusippus' programme refers to plane numbers, that is to say numbers which can be represented by the figures of plane geometry. They can be divided into two categories: 'sum-numbers' or polygonal numbers, and 'product-numbers' or plane numbers proper. The object of the theories which deal with these two categories is to embrace existing numbers, as far as is possible, in series whose terms all have the common property of being capable of representation by the same figure. The best-known of these series is that of square numbers, which have in common the property of being demonstrable in a square. At this point, since it is explaining how numbers can be generated, arithmetic is bordering on ontology: such a series is always infinite, and the last number in its expression always gives rise to yet a further number possessing the same properties.

By sum-number, or polygonal number, is meant a number resulting from the addition of smaller numbers. All numbers from 3 onwards are therefore sum-numbers. But the mathematicians were, naturally, interested only in those which had some notable property of their own, and reserved this name, in practice, for numbers whose parts form an arithmetical progression: such as 6 (the sum of $1+2+3$) or 22 (the sum of $1+4+7+10$). In fact, the starting point of the sum-numbers just was the series $1+2+3$, etc. Indeed, if we display the successive sums of this series by the lines of points, placed one above another, we shall obtain a series of similar triangles.

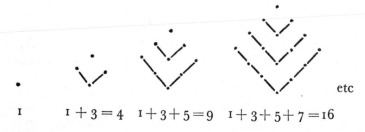

$$1 \qquad 1+2=3 \qquad 1+2+3=6 \qquad 1+2+3+4=10$$

If we construct symmetrical triangles below the bases of these triangles, we shall obtain a new series of sum-numbers:

$$1 \qquad 1+3=4 \qquad 1+3+5=9 \qquad 1+3+5+7=16$$

This is the series of square numbers. Starting now from the same triangles, but making their apex-angles more acute for the sake of convenience, let us construct two symmetrical triangles on two of their sides: we shall then obtain irregular pentagons corresponding to the series of 'pentagonal numbers' 1, 5, 12, 22, etc.:

$$1 \qquad 1+4=5 \qquad 1+4+7=12$$

In other words, for each arithmetical progression there is a corresponding progression of similar polygons, the number of whose sides equals the ratio of the progression increased by 2: the pentagon for the progression of ratio 3, the hexagon for the progression of ratio 4, and so on. This is the theory of polygonal numbers contained in the chapter on plane numbers.

The chapter on solid numbers, which will not be explained here, set out a theory analogous to the theory of sum-numbers. Each solid number in fact is constructed in space in the same way as the plane number in a plane. He begins with the triangular-based pyramid, or tetrahedron, and goes on to other polyhedra, each polyhedron representing the sum of the polygonal numbers associated with the corresponding polygon. Thus the series of tetrahedral numbers 1, 4, 10, 20, etc. corresponds to the series of triangular numbers 1, 3, 6, 10, etc.; and that of pentahedral numbers (pyramid on square base) 1, 5, 14, 30, etc. to that of square numbers 1, 4, 9, 16, etc. Speusippus' text, as summarized by Iamblichus, implies that the analysis of these numbers was normally associated with that of polygonal numbers, of which it formed a sub-section, rather than being tackled separately, as a new branch of arithmetic. On the other hand, it seems likely that Speusippus concentrated on that particular case of the numbers represented by the regular solids, on account of the ontological properties attributed to these figures in the doctrines of the Academy.

Let us return to plane numbers: the second category, that of product-numbers, has still to be explained. The theory of these numbers deals chiefly with the quadrangular figures which result from multiplying together two factors of a non-prime number. As with the other theory, it selected from the whole range of non-prime numbers only those which make up remarkable series. One such example is the sequence of square numbers 1, 4, 9, 16, 25, etc., whose existence was merely noted in the study of sum-numbers, without its special properties being defined. In the search for a principle for generating numbers, this series serves as a basis for calculations applicable also to other series in the same category. It is no longer, in fact, a matter of discovering square numbers by starting from triangular numbers, but one of computing them directly, and extracting from the method of computation a law applicable equally to all product-numbers, or at least to all *oblong* numbers—that is to say, those whose product is the result of the multiplying two factors.

The series of squares envisaged in this calculation makes use of figures in which points are no longer associated with straight or crooked lines, but with the square field which surrounds them:

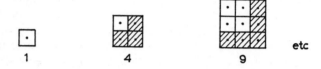

1   4   9   etc

The mathematician's attention is drawn to the strip, shaped like a set-square and hatched diagonally in the above figures, which indicates the number which must be added to each square in order to form the next square. It is immediately apparent that this band, called a *gnomon*, corresponds in the case of squares to an odd number, and that it increases for each square by two units. The series of gnomons of the square is thus identical with the series of odd numbers. Conversely, the sum of any series of successive odd numbers, starting with 1, is always a square number.

The series of square numbers is peculiar in this respect: the figures by which it can be expressed are always similar. On the other hand, when we go from these numbers to oblong numbers, which are represented by rectangles, we can say that the addition of a gnomon to a given rectangle never produces a similar rectangle, but a series of rectangles whose lesser side increases proportionately faster than the greater. Let 6 be the given number: its factors 2 and 3 will increase successively by the addition of the gnomon to 3 and 4, then 4 and 5, then 5 and 6, and so on, forming rectangles which approach more and more nearly towards the square.

So, while the series of squares illustrates the principle of *the same*, that of rectangles illustrates that of *the other*. On this theme of the generation of *the same* and of the generation of *the other*, of *permanence* and *transformation*, of *stability* and *corruption*, and finally of *being* and *becoming*, the philosophy

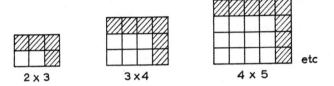

2 x 3   3 x 4   4 x 5   etc

and the physics of the Academy developed unlimited variations. The whole of Plato's *Timaeus*, for example—the dialogue in which the philosopher established by a definitive text his vision of the creation of the universe—is built up on the single opposition which he stated in the following formula:

> Between the indivisible Existence that is ever in the same state and the divisible Existence that becomes in bodies, [the creator] compounded a third form of Existence composed of both . . . intermediate between that kind of them which is indivisible and the kind that is divisible in bodies. (35 A)

As a matter of mathematical research, the analysis of oblong numbers appears to have been developed fully only after Euclid, but by Plato's time certain laws had already been discovered. It was known, for example, that the sum of any series of successive even numbers starting from 2 (say $2 + 4 + 6$ etc.) is always an oblong number whose factors differ by 1 (1×2, 2×3, 3×4, etc.). The analysis of square numbers was directed towards the theory of proportional squares of which several theorems survive in Books VIII and IX of Euclid, for example the following:

> Between two square numbers there is one mean proportional number, and the square has to the square the

ratio duplicate of that which the side has to the side. (*Elem*. VIII, Prop. 11)

The first numbers which confirm this theory are 4, 6 and 9: 4 is to 6 as 6 is to 9. The converse is also stated in Euclid:

If three numbers be in continued proportion, and the first be square, the third will also be square. (*Elem*. VIII, Prop. 22)

These two theorems are moreover regarded solely as particular cases. Since before Plato the theory had included all the proportional relations among plane numbers. It had treated certain solid numbers in a parallel manner. Thus Plato already knew the theorem expressed as follows by Euclid:

Between two cube numbers there are two mean proportional numbers, and the cube has to the cube the ratio triplicate of that which the side has to the side. (*Elem*. VIII, Prop. 12)

The famous Delian Problem, which asks for a method for constructing, with geometrical instruments, a cubic altar having a volume double that of a given cubic altar, is directly relevant to this theorem. It is therefore not surprising that most of the solutions proposed came from the Academy or its immediate neighbourhood. We shall have occasion to return to this point in connection with Eudoxus.

Ontological arithmetic and axiomatic arithmetic

While the theory dealing with the generation of numbers appears productive to us today, as paving a way for the discovery of numbers satisfying certain given conditions, it was not equally so for Plato's most faithful disciples. Aristotle, for instance, declares that Xenocrates and Speusippus took an interest in it only with an eye to a knowledge of realities already existing in the world of becoming (*Metaph*. 1091ᵃ 25). The conflict between the two attitudes adopted by mathematicians towards the study of geometry, that which sees in every new truth the solution of a *problem* and that which makes every truth an eternal truth and the object of a *theorem*, exists also in arithmetic. It did not, to our knowledge, leave its mark in the form of polemical works, perhaps because the tension between the two trends was less marked than in geometry, or because the major advances in the science of numbers had been achieved before the mathematicians had become aware of the difference between axiomatic arithmetic and ontological arithmetic. It is no less a fact that the direction of their research divided them, and that the theories developed by the supporters of the two trends clearly revealed the opposition between their principles. At the time of Plato's death, as we shall see, they became irreconcilable.

Let us begin with the orthodox disciples of Plato. While the problems about numbers drew forth floods of ink from their reed-pens, none of their theories strikes us as more typically ontological than does that of Speusippus. This last is known to us through a long extract from the second part of his treatise *On the Pythagorean Numbers*, frequently quoted above. While the first part summarized the state of knowledge in the science of numbers, with an eye to expounding exhaustively the procedures for generating them, the second and more individual part was devoted to the analysis of the number 10 setting out to demonstrate how, by this number, the perfection of the universe was fulfilled. Twenty lines of quotation will be enough to establish, without any commentary, both the retrograde character of an inquiry which falls back from determinate quantities to their supposed ontological principles, and the sterility of an analysis which wears itself out shuffling the same ideas in every direction, instead of developing new ones:

> The number 10 is a completely perfect number. It is the proper and natural conclusion of our different methods of counting—as much for us Greeks as for the rest of humanity, and that without any arbitrary preference on our part. Indeed, it is the only one to possess several properties worthy of such a perfect number, and furthermore several of the properties it possesses are ones

which every perfect number must contain. In the first place, it must be an even number, in order to contain an equal quantity of even numbers and odd numbers, and not an unequal quantity: since the odd always comes before the even, if the final number was not even there would be one odd number too many. Secondly, it must contain as many prime numbers and non-composite numbers as secondary and composite ones. Now the number 10 satisfies this condition, which is not the case for any smaller number—though several larger numbers do, such as 12 and some others, of which however 10 is the *pythmen* [the decimal root: the others are 12 and 14]: to be the first to possess this property, and the smallest of those which possess it is a token of perfection. And it is certainly a special feature of this number that one finds in it, the first of its kind, composite numbers and non-composite numbers in equal quantity. Add to this that it contains as many sub-multiples as it does multiples of these sub-multiples; up to 5 for sub-multiples, from 6 to 10 for multiples—leaving aside 7, which is neither a sub-multiple nor a multiple, and 4, which is a multiple of 2, so that equality is preserved. Thirdly, ratios of all kinds are comprised in the number 10: the equal, the lesser, the greater, the *epimoros* $(9 + {}^9/_9 = 10)$ and the other varieties, as well as linear, plane and solid numbers, seeing 1 stands for the point, 2 for the line, 3 the triangle and 4 the pyramid $(1 + 2 + 3 + 4 = 10)$.

Over and against this conception of arithmetical research, on whose horizon loom considerations about 'qualities' and what Plato calls 'essences', stands the purely quantitative arithmetic implied in the definition of a number put forward by Eudoxus: a 'determinate multitude'. During Speusippus' time, this arithmetic gave birth to at least two theories which deserve to be noted here, the theory of means and the theory of perfect numbers.

Means arise out of the study of series. This name was applied to groups of numbers in which a middle number turned out to be in a certain sense equidistant between two other numbers, one smaller, the other greater. Up to Eudoxus' time, only three means were known, and the theory about them was apparently formulated by Archytas between 390 and 370 (see p. 180). They are as follows:

1. The arithmetic mean, when of three terms, the *difference* between the first and the second is the same as the difference between the second and the third; for example the number 1 in the mean 1.2.3;

2. The geometric mean, when of the three terms, the *ratio* of the first to the second is the same as the ratio of the second to the third; for example $\frac{1}{2}$ in the mean 1.2.4;

3. The harmonic mean, when the three terms are such that the *differences* between the first extreme and the middle term, and between the middle and third terms represent the same fraction of their respective extremes: for example $\frac{1}{3}$ in the mean 3.4.6.

Instead of concentrating his attention, as Archytas, Plato and the philosophers of the Academy had done, on the presence of these means in Nature, for example in the field of harmony, Eudoxus concerns himself with mathematical properties of this concept of means, and soon discovers three new series possessing analogous properties:

1. *The subcontrary harmonic mean*, in which the *difference* between the first and the second terms and that between the second and the third represent the same fraction of the opposite extreme term, for example $\frac{1}{2}$ in the mean 2.5.6 (the difference between 2 and 5 is half 6, that between 5 and 6 half 2);

2. *The first subcontrary geometric mean*, in which the *ratio* of the smaller to the greater difference equals the ratio of the first extreme to the middle term, for example $\frac{1}{2}$ in the mean 2.4.5 (the difference between 4 and 5 is in the same ratio to the difference between 2 and 4 as the first extreme 2 is to the middle term 4);

3. *The second subcontrary geometric mean*, in which the *ratio* of the smaller to the greater difference equals the ratio of the middle to the second extreme term, for example $\frac{2}{3}$ in the mean 1.4.6 (the difference between 4 and 6 is in the same ratio to the difference between 1 and 4 as the middle term 4 is to the second extreme 6).

Neither acoustics, nor astronomy, nor any other physical

science provide any experimental support for these new relations: one no longer looks for them in Nature. The merit of Eudoxus is that of having isolated what one might call the 'rationale' of the mean—that is to say, what makes it a mean and not simply a series—and of having used this rationale in order to produce novel kinds of means.

The other theory to be considered here is that of the 'perfect numbers'. Like the theory of means, this dates from later than the Pythagorean speculations and, like it, based itself on the results of these speculations—in this case, on the theory of sum-numbers. Starting, in fact, from the observation that every number greater than one is always a sum and sometimes the product of smaller numbers, this new theory aims at discovering numbers in which these two properties are combined in curious combinations. In so doing, it abandons not only all ontological pretensions, but even all reference to the figured numbers of the Pythagoreans: it works with purely arithmetical ideas. Among these curious numbers, the class of perfect numbers is only one of the most interesting; antiquity recognized more of them, from at least as early as Plato's time.

The perfect number is defined as a number whose factors, when added to each other starting from 1, generate the very number whose factors they are. It is accordingly at the same time the sum and the product of these factors. Eudoxus' contemporaries had probably already discovered the four first numbers that fulfil this double condition, out of the twelve identified up to the present. They are:

$$6 = 1 + 2 + 3$$
$$28 = 1 + 2 + 4 + 7 + 14$$
$$496 = 1 + 2 + 4 + 8 + 16 + 31 + 62 + 124 + 248$$
$$8128 = 1 + 2 + 4 + 8 + 16 + 32 + 64 + 127 + 254 + 508 +$$
$$1016 + 2032 + 4064$$

From this period, also, there dates in all probability the famous theorem with which Euclid's three books on arithmetic conclude:

If as many numbers as we please beginning from a unit be set out continuously in double proportion, until the sum of all becomes prime, and if the sum multiplied into the last make some number, the product will be perfect. (*Elem.* IX, Prop. 36)

Here, very much abbreviated, is Euclid's elegant demonstration, using the number 496 as illustration:

Let $\quad\quad\quad a+2a+4a+\ldots m$
be the first group of factors of the perfect number after 1 (*viz.* 2+4+8+16).

Let $\quad\quad\quad e+2e+4e+\ldots n$
be the remainder of these factors, beginning with e, which is the sum of the first group of factors and is a prime number (31+62+...248)

We then have: $\dfrac{m}{a}=\dfrac{n}{e}$ $\left(\dfrac{16}{2}=\dfrac{248}{31}\right)$

So $\quad\quad\quad an=em$ (2×248=31×16)
In other words, the perfect number an (2×248=496) is equal to the product of the sum e (31) of the first series of factors (1 + 2 + 44+ ...) multiplied by the last of those factors m (16).

II. We also have:
$$\frac{2e-e}{e}=\frac{n-e}{e+2e+4e+\ldots}\left(\frac{62-31}{31}=\frac{248-31}{31+62+\ldots}\right)$$
The difference between the first two terms of a geometrical progression $(2e-e)$ is in the same ratio to its first term (e) as the difference between the last and its first terms $(n-e)$ is to the sum of all the terms preceding the last $(e+2e+4e+\ldots)$.

Simplified: $\dfrac{n-e}{e+2e+4e+\ldots}=1$ or $n-e=e+2e+4e+\ldots$

Now by definition $\quad e=1+a+2a+4a+\ldots$
$\quad\quad\quad\quad\quad\quad (31=1+2+4+8+16)$
Therefore $n=1+a+2a+4a+\ldots+m+e+2e+4e+\ldots$
$\quad\quad (248=1+2+4+8+16+31+62+124)$
But by definition $a=2$
Therefore $an=2n$ which is the perfect number in question
So $\quad 2n=1+a+2a+4a+\ldots+m+e+2e+4e+\ldots+n$
It is thus proved that the perfect number $2n$ is equal to the sum of its factors starting from 1.

III. It remains to prove by a very simple argument that e (31) must be a prime number.

If e were not a prime number, it could be broken down into factors. As it is itself a member of the totality of factors of the perfect number, its own factors would then be interspersed between the series of preceding factors. In that case, this series would no longer be a regular geometrical progression in double proportion and demonstrations I and II would no longer be possible. The number e must therefore be a prime number.

Q.E.D.

As we can see, the author of the theorem and its proof worked in I from the theory of proportions, in II from a property of numbers in geometrical progression, and in III from a property of prime numbers. He begins therefore from the point where his predecessors, preoccupied only with establishing laws for the generation of numbers, had ended their investigations. In this he shows himself to be a mathematician of the new school, like Eudoxus faced with the theory of means. If from this theorem we go back to Speusippus's expatiations about the number 10, the distance separating their respective results is astonishing. No reflections about the principles underlying the two arithmetics represented by these examples could speak more clearly than do the examples themselves.

III

Geometry I : Theaetetus

How much was known about geometry at the time when Plato founded the Academy? As we have seen, Eudemus credits Hippocrates of Chios with publishing the first collection of *Elements*. This famous mathematician is known to us chiefly for an attempt to solve the problem of squaring the circle, which resulted in a perfectly correct squaring of the lines bounded by two arcs of a circle. Thanks to Eudemus, we still have almost the complete demonstration, from which we can get an exact idea of the amount of knowledge collected together into his *Elements*. To this can be added the evidence of later mathematicians known to us by virtue of their most original discoveries: Antiphon the Sophist, Democritus, Theodoros of Cyrene, Theaetetus, Archytas. From all this information, the following picture emerges.

All the ordinary figures of plane geometry are identified, from the triangle up to the circle. The three types of angle and the corresponding triangles have already been given their names, as have the different quadrangular figures and all the polygons. The procedure for calculating areas is already understood, except in the case of the circle where approximations are still employed. The constructions for these figures, including the pentagon, are demonstrated.

The conditions governing the equality of angles, triangles and polygonal figures in general, as well as arcs, sectors and segments of the circle have been recognized. The same is true of the conditions governing the similarity of most of these objects.

As for the relations between the various parts of a figure, Pythagoras's theorem is already known, and in addition the relations of inequality between the sides—or the squares on the sides—of non-right-angled isosceles triangles. In this same section are found proportional relations: areas proportional to the squares on their sides, circles proportional to the squares on their diameters. These relations are known and proved. They also knew how to construct a mean proportional between two given segments of a straight line.

Finally, in stereometry, the procedures for calculating volumes are generally known, but the relations between solids are only just beginning to be explored. Democritus has proved that the volume of a pyramid is equal to a third of the volume of a prism having the same base and the same height. He also knows that a cone equals a third of a cylinder of equal base and height, but is unable to prove it except by starting from the pyramid and the cylinder and passing to the limit. Sphaeric, i.e. the definition of the parts of a sphere and the study of their properties, has been given a name by Archytas, but it is impossible to say how far it has been pursued: no doubt it was treated as an appendage to astronomy.

If we leave aside the identification, construction and calculation of the areas of figures, this geometry directed all its efforts towards one goal: the study of relations. Even the classical problems of squaring the circle and duplicating the cube were traced back to problems about relations, the one being presented as the calculation of an area and the other as a problem of construction. In both these cases, moreover, the study of relations took the place of the real object of the problem—to calculate the area of a circle, or the diagonal of a cube—for the very reasons which led to the development of this branch of geometry: the impossibility of expressing certain required quantities by means of integers or rational numbers alone. Using geometrical relations, problems which were not susceptible of arithmetical solutions could be satisfactorily solved. So, the first problem referred to in one of Plato's dialogues, the problem of the *Meno*, turns out to be nothing other than a problem which involves using geometrical figures to circumvent an irrational number: the side of a square whose area is double that of one with sides two feet long has for its length an irrational number—$\sqrt{8}$—which can be represented by the diagonal of the initial square. True, approximations to certain square roots had been suggested. From before the foundation of the Academy the value of $\sqrt{2}$ could be calculated by systematic approximation, using what were known as *side-numbers* and *diameter-numbers*, the operation of extracting the square root (a procedure not yet known) being replaced in this case by one involving the division of one number by another number, for example 17 by 12. But the requirements of mathematical theory were not met by such procedures, and geometry seemed to offer more favourable ground.

The obstacle presented by irrationality was not clearly recognized before—roughly speaking—the foundation of the Academy. Even at that time, it was appreciated only in the case of square roots, or diagonals incommensurable with the sides of the square which they divide. For the square with side 1 unit, the diagonal being necessarily shorter than 2 and longer than 1, it was easy to show that it was irreducible to any unit whatever: the proof followed from the very terms in which the problem was posed. But there was no general proof of the incommensurability of the diagonals of squares with their sides. Around 400 Theodorus of Cyrene had been able to prove that the roots of the first seventeen numbers, except those of 1, 4, 9 and 16, 'are incommensurable with one'. Plato, who tells us about it in the *Theaetetus*, does not describe his argument, but insists that Theodorus had dealt separately with every square and had been unable to establish a general rule.

That, then, was the point which this crucial branch of mathematics had reached when Theaetetus in his turn embarked on it, and undertook to set up a general theory of irrationality. This mathematician, the originality of whose discoveries marks him as one of the greatest of all time, is also the first whose personal appearance is slightly known to us, thanks to the dialogue which Plato dedicated to him. Born around 414, the son of one of the richest and most noble patricians of Attica, Euphronius of Sunium, he was given at Athens the standard education for young men of his standing, dividing his time between the gymnasium and the sophists. A visit by Theodorus of Cyrene to Athens—or by Theaetetus to Cyrene—determined his vocation as a mathematician. His tutors having squandered the fortune left him by his father, he taught geometry and astronomy for a time in Heraclea, an important city on the Black Sea. It was probably there that he began his researches on irrationals and on the regular polyhedra. Returning to Athens about 375, he seems to have taken up teaching again; perhaps Plato introduced him into the Academy. In the summer of 369, having been caught up in the general conscription, he was posted to the defence of Corinth, which was threatened by Epaminondas. Wounded in one of his opening engagements, he was taken back first to Piraeus, then to his estate at Erineus, near Eleusis. He died there soon afterwards, less as a result of his wounds than from a serious attack of dysentery contracted in camp in Corinth. Plato has left us a strikingly individual portrait of him, which is something unusual in his work and testifies to his affection for him: he had a turned-up nose and slightly protruding eyes, an uncommonly penetrating mind, was very quick in his thinking, had a remarkable memory, and with all this possessed a gentleness of character which seems to have been the distinguishing mark of his personality.

Irrationals

As the starting point for his work on irrationals, he took Theodorus of Cyrene's proofs.

> Seeing that these square roots were evidently infinite in number, [we tried] to arrive at a single collective term by which we could designate all these roots. . . . We divided number in general into two classes. Any number which is the product of a number multiplied by itself we likened to the square figure, and we called

such a number 'square' or 'equilateral' ... Any intermediate number, such as 3 or 5 or any number that cannot be obtained by multiplying a number by itself, but has one factor either greater or less than the other, so that the sides containing the corresponding figure are always unequal, we likened to the oblong figure, and we called it an oblong number. All the lines which form the four equal sides of the plane figure representing the equilateral number we defined as *length*, while those which form the sides of squares equal in area to the oblongs we called '*roots*' [or 'powers'] as not being commensurable with the others in length, but only in the plane areas to which their squares are equal. And there is another distinction of the same sort in the case of solids. (*Theaetet.* 147 C—148 B)

The definitions suggested in this quotation lead to the following theorem:

The side of the square of a square number is commensurable *in length*, the side of the square of an oblong number is commensurable *in power* (that is to say by way of its *potential* square), but not in length.

By 'commensurable', Theaetetus meant only 'commensurable with one', that is to say, using his representation of numbers by figures, with the side of a square of unit area. He was criticized in antiquity for not having stated his theorem, as Euclid was to do later in his *Elements* (X, 9), in terms which made it clear that incommensurables such as $\sqrt{8}$ and $\sqrt{18}$ were commensurable with one another not only in *power*, but also in *length*, on account of their smaller common factor $\sqrt{2}$.[1] We can however clear him of this criticism since his theorem, as contrasted with Euclid's, was concerned only with the relation between incommensurables and commensurables, and not with those between pairs of incommensurables. One ancient commentator, who probably obtained his information from Eudemus, confirms moreover

1. This criticism is quoted by Pappus in his commentary on Book X of Euclid's *Elements*, preserved only in an Arabic translation (German version by H. Suter, *Abhandlungen zur Geschichte der Naturwissenschaften und der Medizin*, Vol. IV, 1922, p. 21.)

that he stated his conclusions about the incommensurability *in length* of the sides of oblong numbers with an explicit reservation:

> with this reservation, that certain of them are commensurable with certain others.[1]

This clarification of the exact aim of his research helps one to understand better the significance of his finest discovery, the classification of irrationals. Let us refer once again to Eudemus' *History of Geometry:*

> As for the exact distinctions of the incommensurables and the irrationals and the rigorous demonstrations of the propositions to which this theory gives rise, I believe that they were chiefly established by Theaetetus. For he had distinguished squares commensurable in length from those which are incommensurable, and had divided the well-known species of irrational lines after the different means, assigning the *medial* to geometry, the *binomial* to arithmetic, and the *apotomē* to harmony.[2]

To grasp firstly the distinction which Theaetetus established between incommensurables and irrationals, we must start from the theorem which specified the criterion of incommensurability. It comes to us from Euclid:

> If, when the less of two unequal magnitudes is continually subtracted in turn from the greater, that which is left never measures the one before it, the magnitudes will be incommensurable. (*Elem.* X, Prop. 2)

We have already come across the method applied here, that of reciprocal subtraction or *anthyphairesis*, in connection with the theory of the highest common factor (p. 49). But whereas in arithmetic, where one is dealing with fractions, this method made it possible to demonstrate that two numbers have no common factor, if these subtractions have to be continued right down to one, in geometry, if the lengths being compared are incommensurable with one another, the remainders can in theory be subtracted from

1. See preceding footnote.
2. See preceding footnote, p. 13 of the Commentary.

one another successively an unlimited number of times. Theaetetus' demonstration therefore consisted in proving that an infinite series of subtractions is incompatible with the idea of a lowest common measure.

Having specified this criterion and accepted the existence of incommensurable lengths on the basis of Theodorus's incomplete proofs, Theaetetus directed his efforts not towards defining more precisely the irrational character of these lengths or of the arithmetical quantities to which they correspond, but rather towards making them rational by connecting them up as closely as possible with commensurable lengths. In other words, rather than characterizing them negatively, as lengths lacking certain common properties and eluding the grasp of reason, he tried to define them and name them in positive terms. He defines them as *commensurable by their square* and he calls them *powers:* such lengths as these are not, in his view, *irrationals*.

It should be noted in passing that this first stage in his exploration, which impressed Plato so strongly, breaks every link with ontological mathematics. It starts from purely mathematical ideas, disregards the question what entities these ideas might denote, and concentrates on elucidating certain relations. In spite of that, Plato's disciples made use of it, from their own ontological point of view, to express the unity of being and of the ultimate realities. The author of the *Epinomis* may be quoted, defining geometry as 'the science by which numbers not in themselves mutually comparable are made comparable, by relating them to areas' (see p. 27), and so hoping by geometry to get at fundamental realities of the universe to which numbers do not provide the key. But this very deviation only confirms that the theory of incommensurables was generally accepted, less for its definition of incommensurability than on account of the new relations it enabled one to establish. We may approach the next stage of Theaetetus' research, dealing with irrationals, from this point of view and treat it from now on, not as describing novel and curious mathematical entities, but as throwing light on more obscure and intractable relations within the realm of incommensurables.

Contrary to what Eudemus supposed thirty years later, neither Plato in the *Theaetetus* nor Philip in the *Epinomis* thought of irrationals otherwise than as a particular illustration of incommensurability; in the *Hippias Major*, Plato knew them by the same name as ordinary incommensurables: *surds*.

These *surds*, later known simply as irrationals, are three in number. The first, called the *medial*, is the diagonal of a square having an area equal to that of a rectangle bounded by a *length a* and a *power b*, that is to say by one commensurable straight line and another incommensurable straight line, for example, 1 and $\sqrt{2}$. So if ab is the area of this square, and m its medial, we have

$$m^2 = ab$$

and

$$m = \sqrt{ab}$$

As Eudemus wrote in the passage quoted above, the medial is assigned by Theaetetus to the geometric mean: our equation shows that he means by this that it *is* the geometric mean between the two given lines a and b. But what Eudemus does not say is that Theaetetus had sought after the medial in order to establish a relationship between an incommensurable and a commensurable, a relationship which he could express, for example, in these terms:

A *length* is to a *power* as their product is to the square of the power.

For if

$$m^2 = ab$$

it follows also that

$$\frac{a}{b} = \frac{m^2}{b^2}$$

but

$$m^2 = ab$$

whence the required identity

$$\frac{a}{b} = \frac{ab}{b^2}$$

This identity is interesting, as expressing an incommensurable ratio in commensurable terms and as permitting it to be represented by means of a geometrical figure. Euclid, who incorporated Theaetetus' theory in Book X of the *Elements*, suggests the following figure (Prop. 21):

The second and third irrationals are called the *binomial* and the *apotomē* respectively. The binomial is formed by adding a commensurable to an incommensurable, so that it was called in Greek the 'two-named' line. The apotomē is the difference between a commensurable and an incommensurable, hence its Greek name 'amputation'.

According to Theaetetus, the binomial belongs to the category of arithmetic means. Indeed, suppose *a* be a given *length* and *b* a *power*, their arithmetic mean *m* will be equal to

$$\frac{a + b}{2}$$

whose properties are obviously the same as those of $a + b$, which is the binomial.

It is not so easy to grasp in what respect, to follow Theaetetus again, the apotomē belongs to the category of harmonic means. Algebraically, this mean could be expressed by the equation

$$m = \frac{2ab}{a+b}$$

or $$m(a+b) = 2ab$$

This equation could be expressed by Theaetetus as follows:

> The harmonic mean between a *length* and a *power* is one side of a rectangle whose other side is the binomial of this *length* and *power*, and whose area is twice the medial rectangle bounded by this *length* and this *power*.

If this rectangle is twice the medial rectangle, it is in its turn medial, whatever may be the new ratio of its length to its breadth. Now one theorem which Theaetetus had certainly already proved and which Euclid added as an appendix to Book X of the *Elements* says, substantially, the following:

> The medial rectangle whose length is a binomial will have an apotomē as its breadth. (*Elem.* X, Prop. 112)

Since, as we saw above, $m(a+b)$ is this medial rectangle and $a+b$ this binomial, it follows that *m* is this apotomē. Thus it is proved that the harmonic mean between a *length* and a *power* is an apotomē or, to use Theaetetus' own expression, that the harmonic mean *generates* the apotomē.

How did Theaetetus prove the theorem which leads to this conclusion? It would take too long to follow out his demonstration here step by step. We may be content with a summary which simply indicates, in modern terms, the knowledge of which he avails himself.

Let $n(ab)$ be a medial rectangle which is a multiple—or fraction—of the rectangle ab (which will be medial by definition), and let the binomial $a+b$ be its length; now suppose it has been proved that its breadth is the apotomē $a-b$, this rectangle will then be represented by the equation

$$(1) \qquad n(ab) = (a+b)\ (a-b)$$

But we know—and Theaetetus knew also—that the sum of two terms multiplied by their difference is equal to the difference between their squares. So we have:

$$(2) \qquad (a+b)\ (a-b) = a^2 - b^2$$

By comparing (1) and (2), we get

$$(3) \qquad a^2 - b^2 = n(ab)$$

This new equation indicates that the medial rectangle in question is equal to a multiple—or a fraction—of the difference between the square of the *power* and the square of the *length*. This difference being necessarily a whole number, the area of the rectangle in question will be a whole number or an improper fraction, but not an irrational number. Now it can be seen at once that, if its side is a binomial, that is to say the sum of an irrational number and a rational number, it must be multiplied by the difference between this same number (or one of its multiples) and a rational number, which is the very definition of the apotomē, in order that the irrationality should be eliminated in the multiplication. Then, given a rational and $b = \sqrt{B}$ irrational, we have;
either $\quad (a+ \sqrt{B})\ (a- \sqrt{B})\ = a^2 - B$
and so two whole numbers:
or $\qquad (\sqrt{B}+ a)\ (\sqrt{B}-a) = B-a^2$
and so two whole numbers.
There is therefore only one apotomē which could be the breadth of a medial rectangle whose length is a binomial.

Q.E.D.

It will be noticed that this demonstration, like its pre-decessors, demands only an adequate knowledge of the theory of means, the elementary procedures for calculating areas ... and a certain genius. For even if one poses the question as Theaetetus did—namely, 'What is the harmonic mean between a *length* and a *power*?'—the solution can be drawn directly from the definition of the harmonic mean as the ratio of a product to a sum and from the observation that this sum is a binomial. It is not necessary to establish pre-viously all the properties of irrational lengths, still less to distinguish different varieties of these lengths, as Book X of Euclid does in such a masterly way. This complementary study could have been undertaken by one of his successors. For his own part, Theaetetus seems to have intended only to express the different relationships of commensurability holding between a given *length* and a given *power*.

The five regular polyhedra

In stereometry too Theaetetus is responsible for important discoveries. It is to him that we owe the original construc-tions of the regular octahedron and icosahedron, the pro-cedure for inscribing them in a sphere, and the discovery of the relations between the edges of the regular solids and the diameter of the circumscribing sphere. The collection of theorems on this theme makes up the thirteenth book of Euclid's *Elements*, but the constructions proposed do not agree with the evidence in Plato's *Timaeus*, and we must recognize that in certain respects the theory developed between Theaetetus and Euclid. The intermediate author between them could have been the mathematician Hermo-timus of Colophon, who is supposed to have 'carried further investigations already opened up by Eudoxus and Theaetetus and discovered many propositions of the *Elements*' (see p. 40). Eudoxus also contributed to the theory of solids and at least one of his theorems reappears in Book XIII of Euclid.

If the evidence of the *Timaeus* is applicable to Theaetetus, it seems that he had constructed all his figures, except the cube and the dodecahedron, by starting from the right-angled triangle 'whose hypotenuse is twice as long as the shorter of the sides forming the right angle' (54 D). Four equilateral triangles each made up of six of these triangles gave him the four faces of the first solid, the pyramid with a triangular base. Eight equilateral triangles made up of the same right-angled triangles form the eight faces of the octahedron, which is obtained by joining together at the base two pyramids with square bases. Finally twenty equilateral triangles form the icosahedron, for which the construction is given below. Why begin these constructions with a right-angled triangle, when an equilateral triangle would do as well? Because, by a simple application of Pythagoras's theorem, it provided Theaetetus with the commensurability relation by means of which he could then determine the centre of the solid under construction and calculate the radius of the circumscribed sphere as a function of its edge.

Let us here consider the case of the tetrahedron.

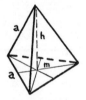 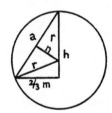

Let m be the median of one of the faces, a the edge, h the height of the tetrahedron; let r be the radius of the circumscribed sphere and n the perpendicular drawn from the centre of this sphere to one of the edges. We then have:

(1) by constructing the faces from right-angled triangles,

$$\frac{m}{a} = \frac{\sqrt{3}}{2}$$

(2) because h meets m at a point $\frac{2}{3}$ along it,

$$h^2 = a^2 - \left(\frac{2}{3}m\right)^2$$

so by combining (1) and (2)

$$h^2 = a^2 - \left(\frac{a\sqrt{3}}{3}\right)^2 = \frac{2a^2}{3}$$

and

$$h = a\sqrt{\frac{2}{3}}$$

(3) from the similarity of the

triangles $h\ a\ \dfrac{2m}{3}$ and $\dfrac{a}{2}\ r\ n$ $\qquad r : \dfrac{a}{2} = a : h$ or $r = \dfrac{a^2}{2h}$

so by combining (2) and (3) $\qquad r = \dfrac{a^2}{2a\sqrt{\dfrac{2}{3}}} = \dfrac{a}{2\sqrt{\dfrac{2}{3}}}$

Expressing this equation in terms of a commensurability relation by way of the squares, and replacing the radius r by the diameter d, we obtain:

since $d = 2r$, $\qquad d = \dfrac{a}{\sqrt{\dfrac{2}{3}}}$

the relation of commensurability $d^2 = \dfrac{3}{2}\,a^2$

This relation is the same as that described by Euclid's theorem:

> The square on the diameter of the sphere is one and a half times the square on the side of the pyramid. (*Elem.* XIII, Prop. 13)

The argument is simpler in the case of the octahedron. As this figure has a square as median base, it is obvious that the centre of the circumscribed sphere coincides with the centre of this square, whose diagonal also becomes the diameter of the sphere. But this diagonal is the hypotenuse of the equilateral right-angled triangle whose two sides are the edges of the octahedron. So Theaetetus had to conclude that

> The square on the diameter of the sphere is double that of the square on the side of the octahedron. (Eucl. *Elem.* XIII, Prop. 14)

The construction of the icosahedron rests on that of the pentagon. The icosahedron can in fact be described as follows: two pyramids with pentagonal bases whose bases are joined the one to the other by a ring having ten faces in the form of equilateral triangles, in such a way that each of the ten triangles has for one of its sides an edge of the base of one pyramid and meets an angle of the base of the other pyramid at its apex. Or again: let us place two pyramids with pentagonal bases opposite one another in such a way that the base-angles of one face of the mid-points of the edges of the other bring them together until the distances separating them is equal to the height of one of the triangular faces and construct new edges joining each angle of the two bases to the two angles of the opposite base facing it: we have then constructed a regular icosahedron.

The construction of the pentagon starting from an isosceles triangle whose base angles are double the angle at the vertex was already known before Theatetetus. But he is perhaps the first to have established that the straight lines joining two successive angles of a pentagon (*cc'* and *dd'* in the figure below) intersect (at point *P* in the figure) in extreme and mean ratio, that is to say in such a way that the smaller segment is to the greater as the greater is to their sum

$$\left(\frac{c}{c'} = \frac{c+c'}{c'}\right).$$

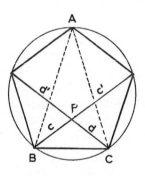

This proportion, famous throughout antiquity, has been known since Leonardo da Vinci's time as the *golden section*. The golden section obtrudes itself during construction of the pentagon starting from the circle which circumscribes it. Without going into further details, we must here recall that the triangle on which the pentagon is constructed (*ABC* in the figure) is itself constructed using a golden section of the radius of this circle. As a consequence of the definition of the section, if we cut the smaller segment out of the larger segment, then the remainder of the larger out of the smaller, then the smaller remainder from the larger remainder, and so on, the smallest remainder will at no stage measure the other—infinite *anthyphairesis* (see p. 43)—Theaetetus had recognized in the relation between the two segments of the section a typical example of irrationality. Furthermore, the removal of an irrational or rather incommensurable segment from a given straight line evidently produced an example of apotomē. Theaetetus thus saw the properties of this irrational as characteristic not only of the golden section in general, but also more particularly of the side of a pentagon as compared with the radius of the circle circumscribed about it. It would take far too long to repeat here the admirable but lengthy demonstration in Euclid Book XIII (Prop. 16), which moreover led on to a classification of the varieties of apotomē—a classification probably still unknown to Theaetetus. It cannot escape the modern reader that, having identified the apotomē relating the circle and the pentagon, Theaetetus was bound to discover the similar relation between the sphere and the icosahedron, although this sphere has a greater radius than the circle for the same pentagonal base. Further, his theorem concluded by asserting that the edge of the pentahedron forms an apotomē with the diameter of the circumscribed sphere.

What is true of the icosahedron is also true of the dodecahedron, Theaetetus' fourth figure. This, indeed, has as its faces twelve pentagons. Its edge, then, like that of the icosahedron, is an apotomē of the diameter of the circumscribed sphere. However, since its construction does not involve the elementary right-angled triangle from which one composed the equilateral triangles constituting the faces of the earlier solids, it occupies a place apart in the series of solids.

As for the cube, neither its construction nor its inscription within a sphere presents any difficulty. The relevant theorem specifies also its relationship to this sphere:

The square on the diameter of the sphere is triple that of the square on the side of the cube. (Eucl. *Elem*. XIII, Prop. 15)

The diameter d of the circumscribed sphere is identical with the diagonal joining two opposite vertices of the cube.

Taken together with the diagonal c on the square face of the cube and the edge a, this diagonal forms a right-angled triangle of which it is the hypotenuse. Therefore:

$$d^2 = a^2 + c^2$$

but c is related to a by the equation:

$$c = 2\sqrt{a^2}$$

whence we deduce that $d^2 = a^2 + (\sqrt{2a^2})^2 = 3a^2$

Q.E.D.

Finally (as indirectly testified by Plato) Theaetetus had proved the theorem with which Euclid Book XIII concludes:

No other figure, besides the said five figures, can be constructed which is contained by equilateral and equiangular figures equal to one another.

It having been established that the sum of the plane angles which make up the solid angle of a three-dimensional figure must be less than four right angles, this condition is evidently fulfilled only by the vertices of less than six equilateral triangles ($6 \times 60° = 360°$), less than 4 squares ($4 + 90° = 360°$) and less than four pentagons ($4 + 98° = 392°$, but $3 \times 98° = 294°$). The vertices of three hexagons already total this limit ($3 \times 120° = 360°$).

Mathematics and physics: from the five solids to the five elements

At the time of writing the chapter in the *Republic* from which

a long extract was quoted above (p. 23), i.e. around 375–
370, Plato deplored the fact that stereometry was still the
preserve of the mathematicians and did not interest philosophers to any extent.

> Even now, despised as the subject is by the public and
> curtailed by students who do not take account of its
> true utility, in spite of everything it is gaining ground,
> thanks to its inherent charm; and it would not be
> surprising if inquiry should succeed in bringing the
> truth to light. (VII 528 C)

From these lines, it appears that Theaetetus' investigations were still only just beginning and that their aim was
not yet clearly visible. However, neither the *Theaetetus*,
written shortly after the mathematician's death, nor the
Sophist or the *Statesman*, in which Plato gives him a role and
which were published about 360, make the slightest allusion
to the significance of his discoveries about the five solids.
Everything went on as though geometers had not recognized
their importance. But soon, Leodamas of Thasos having
completed his demonstrations by a systematic application
of the new method, known as 'analysis', Leon could incorporate them in his *Elements* and so bring them to the attention of a much wider public. Some of the theorems quoted
here as the work of Theaetetus may perhaps go back no
further than these last works. However that may be, Plato
himself only reaped their benefits in the *Timaeus*, that is to
say, around 355.

The *Timaeus* discloses Plato's teachings about the creation
of the universe, the composition of nature, in short, his
physics. Having in the first chapters described the astronomical universe, the motion of the heavenly bodies and the
creation of human beings, the philosopher comes to the
elements of matter, which are to be the subject of a long
analysis. Like most physicists in his time, he distinguished
four such elements: fire, earth, water and air. But how was
one to visualize these elements in space, and as bodies having
volume? Relying on the parallelism for which he was constantly searching, between the hierarchy of material things

79

and the hierarchy of mathematical objects, Plato must have been led to consider geometrical figures and to see in them the likenesses of material things and their underlying substances. So Theaetetus' solids claimed his attention. And they arrived, as we have seen, circumscribed within a sphere: that is, within the perfect shape which Plato believed to be that of the universe. From that point on, how could he deny that they held a privileged position among all the profusion of geometrical bodies?

The first characteristic virtue of the five solids, in Plato's eyes, is their ability 'to divide the whole circumference into equal and similar parts, (55 A). Another characteristic property—and one very unusual in mathematics—is that they compose, not an unlimited group of individual figures, but a species limited to five, whereas the regular polygons inscribed within a circle are infinite in number, likewise the pyramids inscribed in a cone and the prisms inscribed in a cylinder. There is a wonderful coincidence between this property and the fixed number of material elements, which demanded a comparison between them. Yet a difficulty arose here which Plato did not manage to resolve. After deciding to relate each element to one of Theaetetus's solids, he found himself with one solid too many. Fire, on account of the shape of its flame, could easily be compared to the pyramid. It is also, according to Plato, the most tenuous of the elements, just as the pyramid is the slenderest of the solids. Water, on the contrary, is the bulkiest of the elements: it corresponds to the icosahedron. Air, having an intermediate density, corresponds to the third solid with triangular faces: the octahedron, whose number of faces also lies between those of the two figures already allocated. Finally, for analogous reasons, earth is likened to the cube:

> For ... it is the most immobile and the most plastic of bodies [and must be likened to] the figure whose bases are the most stable. (55 E)

What about the dodecahedron? Plato evades the problem of the 'quintessence' ('fifth essence') with a cryptic formula:

> There still remained one construction, the fifth; and the god used it for the whole. (55 C)

This way of escape did not satisfy the unfailing curiosity of his disciples. And indeed, during the years that followed, instead of repeating the master's words, one finds them doing their best to credit him with a very different opinion from that hinted at by the sentence in the *Timaeus*. According to their account, he discovered a fifth element, the 'ether', and as its extreme tenuousness made it—if density was used as a criterion—barely explicable in terms of the dodecahedron, the order of the five bodies had to be modified. Modern historians have wondered whether Plato did perhaps change his mind after the publication of the *Timaeus*, or whether the problem of the fifth element remained under discussion within the Academy, which would seem more likely. One thing remains certain: after Plato's death, this element formed a part of the *credo* bequeathed by the founder to his fellow-disputants, and it gave rise, not only among them but in Aristotle's circle also, to highly original speculations in the fields of theology and metaphysics. However, neither the *Philebus* nor the *Laws*, which are the last extant works of Plato, makes the slightest reference to it.

So far as we are concerned, the theory of the fifth element starts with the *Epinomis*, which was published under Plato's name, as being a faithful account of his doctrine. After recalling the principle

> that there are five material elements . . . namely, fire and water, thirdly air, fourthly earth and fifthly ether, (981 BC)

our pseudo-Plato speaks at length about two of these elements, fire and earth, keeping faithfully to the *Timaeus* and not bringing in his own opinions. Then he goes back to the five elements and suggests ordering them in a new way, according to the criteria which he has just elucidated in the case of the first two:

> Let us now try to say, as clearly as possible and according to the most appropriate view, which elements

occupy the three middle places in the series of five, between fire and earth. After fire, let us put ether and let us suppose that the soul fashions from it a second kind of living things. Finally, the third is formed of water. (984 BC)

As we saw earlier, Speusippus reserved a special place in his treatise *On the Pythagorean Numbers* for the study of the five solids: the whole of the second part.

Then came the five figures which give their shape to the elements of the universe, with their respective properties and their common characteristics, their analogies and their reciprocal relations.

The order of elements in his list is not known. There are certain indications that he began, like Plato, with fire. While claiming to reproduce the ancient Pythagorean doctrine, which he had discovered in a mysterious treatise by Philolaus, he nevertheless did not hesitate to quote Plato as an authority also. For the treatise which came into his possession after his uncle's death had been purchased by him, according to Speusippus, during his visit to Sicily for the fabulous sum of forty *minas* of silver—the price of twenty slaves!—and the *Timaeus* was directly inspired by it. Thus Speusippus too, like the author of the *Epinomis*, resorted to a subterfuge, guaranteeing his claims to orthodoxy by invoking the authority of Plato himself. If the declaration about the five elements traditionally ascribed to Philolaus can be traced back to this miraculous treatise, one can then attribute it with confidence to Speusippus and confirm that, of all such opinions, it adheres most faithfully to the doctrine of the *Timaeus*:

The bodies forming the sphere of the universe are five in number; within the sphere there are fire, water, earth, and air, and the shell of the sphere makes the fifth. (44 B 12)

Finally Xenocrates, in his *Life of Plato*, writes roughly as follows:

Plato divided up living things into categories and parts, and continued these divisions in all sorts of ways until he reached the five elements of all beings, which he called *five figures* and *five bodies:* ether, fire, water, earth and air. (Fr. 51)

Xenocrates, for his part, naturally professed the same opinion. After the apochryphal treatise and the secret document, the biographical memoir in its turn covers the disciple's speculation—just in time—with the authority of the master.

The fact that three of the most devoutly conformist of Plato's followers should claim to be expressing the orthodox doctrine about this particular point, and made use of such stratagems in doing so, is an indication that the theory in question truly represented a central element in the philosophy taught at the Academy from the *Timaeus* on. The evidence of Xenocrates opportunely reminds us that this theory is embodied in a physics which embraces the whole of Nature, and that it makes its appearance at a most delicate juncture: at the point where the world of living things is connected on to the world of matter. This exposed situation is the reason why it was the object of such lively questioning. Furthermore, the bitter controversy between Philip of Opus, Speusippus and Xenocrates illustrates this fundamental principle of Platonism: that mathematics must be studied, not for its own sake, but as leading to an understanding of reality. On this principle, their certainty is absolute: it is not in debate. They could, in fact, have given up their search for a correlative to the fifth solid, and so thrown doubt on all the correlations in the *Timaeus*. But their conviction that the mathematical truth in question governed physical reality also had origins more tenacious even than Plato's teaching: its roots were psychological. It drew its strength from the profound consciousness of an all-embracing harmony, by which life, movement, existence and the cosmic spaces themselves were all alike made subject to the law of Number alone. To underline the point: their conviction was in the first place a matter of feeling rather than

83

reason, and even the *Timaeus*—that basic charter of Platonic physics—must itself be understood entirely, down to its most fantastic speculations, less as a mathematical proof than as a hymn of praise sung by Plato in honour of the divine architect and the perfection of his handiwork.

IV

Geometry II : Eudoxus I

The most celebrated mathematician among Plato's contemporaries became famous for his contributions to three
sciences—geometry, astronomy and geography—but it was
undoubtedly in astronomy that he was led to his most
spectacular discoveries. Although it caused less stir, however,
his work in geometry was equally valuable, and perhaps in
the long run more fruitful. We shall, in fact, see that his
analysis of the solar system, though provoking a salutary
revival in methods of astronomical observation and finding
immediate practical applications, contained the same flaws
as those of his predecessors and did not come one whit nearer
the truth. His theory of proportion, on the other hand, not
only resulted in better proofs of some theorems already known
but also established firmly certain of the principles on which
mathematics is still based today. Moreover, his astronomy was
the first to be subordinated entirely to the laws of geometry,
and a geometry which was no longer, like Pythagorean
geometry, just a harmony of circles and spheres, but the
proper application of mathematical forms and relations to
the movements of the stars.

The biography left to us by antiquity gives us a fairly full
account of his life. The exact date of his birth is at present in
dispute: according to contradictory information, it can be
varied twenty years earlier or later. Most historians prefer
the earlier chronology, according to which he was born

around 408 and was some forty years old in 368[1], so that
Plato would have come under his influence. But an unquestioned testimony assures us that he died at the age of
fifty-three, whilst a quotation from his treatise on geography
makes a reference to the death of Plato, which occurred, as
we know, in 347: on this account, he must have been born
after 400. This evidence favours the later chronology, which
puts his birth about 391 and death about 338. Accepting
these limits, which are adopted here because they agree with
the information given by Eudemus (see p. 40), Eudoxus
becomes a contemporary of Plato's pupils, and his chief
works appear too late for the philosopher to have been able
to give them much attention.

Devoted for several generations to the medical profession,
Eudoxus' family sent him to study, up to the age of twenty-
three, at the excellent medical school of Cnidus, which was
a recognized rival to that founded by Hippocrates at Cos.
He became assistant to the doctor, Theomedon, and had the
good fortune to accompany him to Athens in 368 for a visit
lasting two months. Theomedon found him lodgings in the
Piraeus, but his appetite for knowledge was such (his
biographers tell us) that he made every day the double
journey between the two towns, of four or five miles each
way, in order to attend lectures by the great philosophers.
There is no doubt that he met Plato there, but their difference
in age and status must have put a great distance between
them. On his return to Cnidus, he probably settled down to
practise his art, at the same time as completing his education.
Several years later, in 365 or 364, he went to Egypt with
another doctor, Chrysippus. On this occasion he was entrusted by Agesilaus, King of Sparta, who was on a diplomatic mission to the eastern seaboard of the Aegean, with a
letter for the Pharaoh Nectanebo I, to whom Agesilaus
proposed to offer the help of Spartan mercenaries against the
King of Persia. Eudoxus having been introduced by means

1. This date is linked with the discovery of certain 'curved lines' used in
the solution of the Delos problem. This problem was itself used to establish
an artificial contemporaneity between Archytas, Eudoxus and Plato. This
dates back through the chronographer Apollodorus of Athens to Eratosthenes
(see below, p. 114).

of this letter into the presence of the sovereign, the latter put him in touch with certain priests at Heliopolis, and there he remained for fourteen months, living partly on their hospitality, and partly on an allowance given to him on his departure from Cnidus by some friends wealthier than himself. He took advantage of this time to make numerous observations, both of the rising of the Nile and of the southern constellations unknown to the Greeks. He made himself familiar with the Egyptian calendar and had his hosts explain to him the legend of Isis and Osiris as well as certain curious aspects of their system of worship.

Returning to Asiatic Greece, he lost no time in opening a school at Cyzicus, an important stopping-place between the Hellespont and the Bosphorus. His success is borne out by the large number of pupils whom he trained there, and by the distinction of being invited to meet the ostentatious tyrant Mausolus, the same man whose name was immortalized by the famous Mausoleum. In Cyzicus he published his first works: the *Phaenomena*, in which he described the constellations together with their risings and settings; then, very likely, a treatise on the methods for observing the risings of stars; and finally perhaps also his great work *On Speeds* which analyses the movements of the sun, the moon and planets.

Some years before 350 he handed over the direction of his school to one of his pupils and went to live temporarily in Athens, taking several pupils with him. This move can partly be explained by the attraction exerted at this period by the great Athenian masters, notably at the Academy. But it could have been due also to financial difficulties, for it happened to coincide with a failure of the Cyzicus currency, which until that time had dominated the markets of the Aegean and the Black Sea. Shortly after his arrival in Athens, important political changes at his native town of Cnidus called for his attention. Taking advantage of deep dissensions within the ruling oligarchy, the people had overthrown the government and set up a democracy. This incident took place round about 350 and was followed by a complete transplantation of the city of Cnidus to a site nearer to the coast. Wishing to provide themselves with a constitution, the Cnidians sent an appeal to Eudoxus (then about forty years old) which he accepted. So he returned to his native land, drew up the required legislation, and was repaid for this with great honours, the memory of which was perpetuated by an official inscription.

Based from now on in Cnidus, he taught a varied programme within the framework of the school of medicine. He continued his astronomical observations as vigorously as ever, and for this purpose built himself an observatory which could still be seen two centuries later. He died, still fully active, in 338. It was at Cnidus that he published a revised edition of his *Phaenomena* under the title of *The Mirror* and, most important, the seven books of his *Tour of the Earth*. Antiquity also attributed to him a number of other books on a great variety of subjects, but their titles have not come down to us, except for a didactic poem in epic verse, entitled *Astronomy*, and a work of doubtful authenticity, the *Dialogues of Dogs*, which seems to have been a collection of Egyptian stories.

Geometry

The book titles mentioned in this biography, which are the only ones known to us, throw no light at all on his work as a geometer. Does it follow that this did not take the form of books, and that antiquity knew of it only from the oral testimony of his pupils? Or did he incorporate his theories into one or other of his treatises on astronomy? The theorems on proportions, for example, underlie the calculations for determining the periods of the planets. The theorems on proportional spheres might have found an application in the same context. Yet against these two possibilities stands the fact that his expositions of these theorems would necessarily have included preliminary definitions followed by theorems necessarily connected one to another: this is the very structure of geometrical theories. So the evidence strongly suggests that somewhere in his writings, whether as a self-contained work or as one chapter in a treatise on celestial mechanics, were to be found fully developed treatments of certain geometrical subjects. On the other hand, we must dismiss the idea that he might have written a complete set of *Elements,* since Eudemus does not attribute this to him. Rather, we may suppose that he used those of his predecessors, that is to say Leon's handbook at least, and perhaps also the one by Hippocrates of Chios.

The discoveries in geometry which Eudemus attributes to Eudoxus are as follows:

1. 'He was the first to increase the number of the so-called general theorems' means that he composed the first general theory of proportions;

2. 'He also added three other mean proportionals to the three already known' refers to a chapter in arithmetic already dealt with in its place above. (p. 58);

3. 'He multiplied the theorems which originated with Plato about the section' certainly refers to the golden section;

4. '. . . applying to them the method of analysis' refers only to the demonstrations on the golden section, not to the whole of his works.

To these subjects of study can be added the theorems on the proportionality of spheres and a solution to the problem of duplicating the cube, about which we are told by Archimedes and Eratosthenes respectively. If we leave aside the reference to the use of the method of analysis, which is not directly relevant to his discoveries, five distinct theories remain, of which one, that on means, has to do with arithmetic as much as geometry. Whether he expounded them orally, inserted them into his astronomical works or published them separately, they represent so important a collection as to qualify him to bear, and bear proudly, the title of geometer.

Theory of proportion

We have already come across theorems relating to proportions in two connections. In arithmetic we saw that the theory of reciprocal subtraction—*antanairesis* or *anthyphairesis*—enables one to determine whether or not two given numbers are prime to one another, thus establishing their ratio, and that it gave rise to the idea that two pairs of numbers are proportional when in each pair the *anthyphairesis* consists of corresponding sequences of operations carried out in the same order. In Theaetetus' geometry, we saw also that the commensurability or incommensurability of two segments of a straight line is established by an *anthyphairesis*: if the subtraction of the segments continues indefinitely, they are incommensurable; if it ends by the measurement of the greater segment by the smaller, they are commensurable. It is more difficult, in practice, to base a law of proportion on this, as a measurement is always a delicate matter, but we must admit that, as in arithmetic, this theory established that a shared *anthyphairesis* defines two pairs of segments as proportional. In plane geometry, and still more in the geometry of space, this procedure could no longer be applied, except on a purely theoretical basis. It had obviously been tailored solely to the needs of arithmetic, and its extension to other fields of mathematics came up against serious difficulties. It was necessary to find a procedure of more general application: this was the aim of Eudoxus's theory.

As Aristotle pointed out, this generalization begins with the definition of proportion. To define it by 'same *anthyphairesis*' was to restrict it to arithmetic:

> Another case is the theorem about proportion, that you can take the terms alternately (i.e. *alternando*). This theorem used at one time to be proved separately for numbers, for lines, for solids, and for times, though it admitted of proof by one demonstration. But because there was no name comprehending all these things as one, I mean numbers, lengths, times, and solids, which differ in species from one another, they were treated separately. Now, however, the proposition is proved universally: for the property did not belong to the subjects *qua* lines or *qua* numbers, but *qua* having a particular character which they are assumed to possess universally. (*Analyt. Post.* 74ᵃ17)

It has been known for a long time that this passage refers to Eudoxus' theory and contrasts it with earlier theories. By 'now', however, Aristotle means less the actual work of Eudoxus than the (then) latest *Elements*, i.e. those of Theudius of Magnesia. Let me add that the inclusion of 'times', in the list of mathematical objects, refers to astronomy and so confirms that this theory had found an application in the computation of planetary revolutions, which probably originated in Eudoxus' treatise on heavenly mechanics.

The ancient commentators on Euclid's *Elements* tell us that Book V, which reproduces the theory of proportion, is derived in the main from Eudoxus:

> This book is said to be by the mathematician Eudoxus of Cnidus, who lived in Plato's time. Nevertheless it is attributed to Euclid, and this is not a trick. There is in fact nothing to prevent its having been someone else's work, as regards the invention of the theory: but the synthetic exposition of the material in the form of elements, and the adaptation of the elements thus arranged to other parts of the work are, in the general opinion, the work of Euclid. (Fr. D 32)

According to Aristotle's evidence, the theorem on proportion *alternando* (after exchange of corresponding terms) represented the culminating point of the theory. If we act on this hint—which is in other respects rather weak—we can eliminate from the Euclidean version a whole series of definitions and theorems contrary to Aristotle's testimony. But Aristotle also makes use on occasion of theorems which in Euclid succeed that of 'exchanged terms' (*alternando*), and this shows that these are early in date. So this testimony poses an insoluble problem; which of these theorems go back to Eudoxus and which come only from Theudius? For the purposes of this account the wider solution will be adopted, which involves taking into account all the theorems attested by Aristotle, and supplementing them by those from Euclid which are indispensable for the progress of the argument. This approach may have the disadvantage of exaggerating the contribution of Eudoxus, but it has the advantage of giving as complete an idea as possible of the progress in geometry made as a result of his stimulus.

The five definitions which made possible the generalization of the theory of proportion are as follows:

I. A ratio is a sort of relation in respect of size between two magnitudes of the same kind. (*Elem.* V, Def. 3)

II. Magnitudes are said to have a ratio to one another which are capable, when multiplied, of exceeding one another. (*Elem.* V, Def. 4)

III. Proportion is the sameness of ratios. (Arist. *Eth. Nicom.* 1131ᵃ31)

IV. Magnitudes are said to be in the same ratio, the first to the second and the third to the fourth, when, if any equimultiples whatever be taken of the first and third, and any equimultiples whatever of the second and fourth, the former equimultiples alike exceed, are alike equal to, or alike fall short of, the latter equimultiples respectively taken in corresponding order. (*Elem.* V, Def. 5)

V. When, of the equimultiples, the multiple of the first magnitude exceeds the multiple of the second, but the multiple of the third does not exceed the multiple of the fourth, then the first is said to have a greater ratio to the second than the third has to the fourth. (*Elem.* V., Def. 7)

These definitions, which are in some respects a little complicated, call for a word of explanation. In the first, 'relation in respect of size' specifies the distinctive property of the term chosen by Eudoxus in order to embrace all mathematical notions under a single noun: *magnitude*. If this term had been *number*, he would have spoken of 'relation in respect of quantity'. In the same definition, 'of the same kind' is a translation of the Greek *homogenēs*: this in no way denies the general scope of the theory of proportion, for the word implies only that mathematical magnitudes are in question, not any kind of magnitude whatever, and this is what Aristotle also means when he speaks of the 'particular character which they are assumed to possess universally' (p. 90).

The second definition looks back towards *anthyphairesis*, but only distantly. Instead of subtracting the two magnitudes from one another, Eudoxus multiplies one of them and satisfies himself that this operation truly increases it. He thus excludes from these relationships not only negative magnitudes, which he does not yet recognize, but also non-mathematical magnitudes or infinitesimal ones. The fourth definition completes the intention of the second, by showing that if the same multiplications, when applied to the corresponding terms of two ratios, result in *equimultiples*—that is to say, multiples of these terms obtained by the same multiplicator, such that their relation to the other term of the same ratio is identical in the two ratios—the two initial ratios are in proportion. In many ways, the idea of 'same *equimultiplication*' recalls that of 'same *anthyphairesis*'; and this was obviously its original inspiration. An axiom quoted by Archimedes served as a link, by proposing addition rather than multiplication, though still without touching on proportions:

> Of unequal lines, unequal surfaces, or unequal solids, the greater exceeds the less by such a magnitude as is capable, if added continually to itself, of exceeding any magnitude of those which are comparable with one another. (*Quadrat. Parab.* p. 264)

This formulation was envisaged as applying solely to geometrical objects. It therefore represents an intermediate stage between *anthyphairesis*, which is applicable to geometrical magnitudes only with difficulty, and Eudoxus' general definition. Like the latter, however, it already aims at going beyond the distinction between commensurable and incommensurable straight lines, so as to establish relations of proportionality between all straight lines.

Finally, the fifth definition opens up the hitherto unexplored field of inequalities. For the first time in the history of the exact sciences, a relation as unruly and as contrary to the Greek conception of mathematics as inequality was to be grasped in mathematical terms. This remarkable extension of scope is an incidental consequence of Eudoxus' striving after generality: he wished to include all relations whatever, not only those of equality and similitude. Granted, it is still for him only a matter of defining the notion of 'greater ratio' in relation to that of 'same ratio'; nevertheless he bases on this definition several complementary theorems in which he is undeniably attempting to subject an obstinate relation to the laws of mathematics.

Of the theorems reproduced by Euclid, the first important one is a direct consequence of definition IV:

1. If a first magnitude have to a second the same ratio as a third to a fourth, any equimultiples whatever of the first and third will also have the same ratio to any equimultiples whatever of the second and fourth respectively, taken in corresponding order. (*Elem.* V, Prop. 4)

This theorem can be considered as the reciprocal of definition IV, and proved by simply referring to its terms.

Four theorems follow which, taking definitions IV and V as their starting-point, establish the ratio between two magnitudes and a third:

2. Equal magnitudes have to the same the same ratio, as also has the same to equal magnitudes. (*Elem.* V, Prop. 7)

Let the magnitudes a and b be equal to one another, and let c be a third magnitude.
Consider on the one hand ma and mb, equimultiples of a and b, and on the other hand oc, some multiple of c.
Let us suppose in succession that $ma > oc$, then $ma = oc$, finally $ma < oc$, we shall then have in succession $mb > oc$, then $mb = oc$, finally $mb < oc$

So, by virtue of definition IV $\qquad \dfrac{ma}{oc} = \dfrac{mb}{oc}$

whence, dividing by $\dfrac{m}{o}$, $\qquad \dfrac{a}{c} = \dfrac{b}{c}$

$$\text{Q.E.D.}$$

The second proposition of the theorem is proved similarly, starting from the relations $oc > ma$, $oc = ma$, $oc < ma$.

3. Magnitudes which have the same ratio to the same are equal to one another: and magnitudes to which the same has the same ratio are equal. (*Elem.* V, Prop. 9)

Euclid's demonstration consists in showing that this theorem is the reciprocal of the preceding one.

4. Of unequal magnitudes, the greater has to the same a greater ratio than the less has: and the same has to the less a greater ratio than it has to the greater. (*Elem.* V, Prop. 8)

With this theorem, which is derived from definition V, Eudoxus is embarking on the study of inequalities. The proof is accordingly more complicated, perhaps also clumsier.

Let the magnitudes $a > b$, and let c be a third magnitude; it is required to prove that $\dfrac{a}{c} > \dfrac{b}{c}$. As a and b, being variable magnitudes, have no common measure, Eudoxus starts from a magnitude which depends simultaneously on the two magnitudes in question: $(a-b)$. In this way, any argument having to do with this new magnitude can be applied separately to a and b.

By virtue of definition II, there exists some multiple of $(a-b)$ which exceeds c.

Let $m(a-b)$ be this multiple:

Then $\qquad\qquad m(a-b) > c \qquad\qquad (1)$

From this point on, Eudoxus must consider two cases, according as b is greater or smaller than the magnitude $(a-b)$.

First let $\qquad\qquad a-b < b$

then, by (1), $\qquad\qquad m(a-b) < mb$

Whatever the value of m, there exists by virtue of definition II some multiple of c which exceeds mb. So, if nc is the last multiple of c less than mb (or equal to mb):

we have, firstly $\qquad\qquad mb > nc \qquad\qquad (2)$

then, by increasing n $\qquad mb < (n+1)c$

Therefore, *a fortiori*, $\qquad m(a-b) < (n+1)c$, since we took $a-b < b$

Adding together (1) and (2),

$$m(a-b) + mb > (n+1)c$$

or $\qquad\qquad ma > (n+1)c$

We see, then, that ma is to $(n+1)c$ in a greater ratio than mb is to $(n+1)c$, which can be expressed by the equation

$$\frac{ma}{(n+1)c} > \frac{mb}{(n+1)c}$$

But what is true of equimultiples is true also of the corresponding magnitudes before multiplication: therefore

$$\frac{a}{c} > \frac{b}{c}$$

Q.E.D.

Let us now take $a-b > b$ and proceed by applying the same operations to $(a-b)$ as were previously applied to b; it is clear that we shall once again find equimultiples ma and $m(a-b)$ such that

$$ma > (n+I)c$$

while

$$m(a-b) < (n+I)c$$

But, as we took $a-b > b$, *a fortiori*

$$mb < (n+I)c$$

Hence we conclude as before $\dfrac{a}{c} > \dfrac{b}{c}$

Q.E.D.

The second proposition of the theorem, according to which $\dfrac{c}{b} > \dfrac{c}{a}$, is proved similarly.

5. Of magnitudes which have a ratio to the same, that which has a greater ratio is greater; and that to which the same has a greater ratio is less. (*Elem.* V, Prop. 10)

This theorem is the reciprocal of the previous one.

After the four theorems on the ratios of two magnitudes to a third, there follow three theorems on the relation of two ratios to a third or to a number of other ratios: that is to say, the relation of proportionality.

6. Ratios which are the same with the same ratio are also the same with one another. (*Elem.* V, Prop. 11, Arist. *Meteor.* 376ª22)

Given $\dfrac{a}{b} = \dfrac{c}{d}$ and $\dfrac{e}{f} = \dfrac{c}{d}$, to prove that $\dfrac{a}{b} = \dfrac{e}{f}$. The proof applies definition IV. Eudoxus argues, indeed, in terms of the equimultiples of the given magnitudes, ma, mc, me on the one hand, nb, nd, nf on the other, and shows that the modification introduced by the equimultiples into the first ratio produces identical effects on the third by way of the second. In virtue of definition IV, this identity entails the identity of the ratios under consideration.

A digression is here permissible. Transcribed into algebraic notation, this proof is pointless, since the sign '$=$' serves by itself alone to guarantee that

if $\qquad \dfrac{a}{b} = \dfrac{c}{d}$ and $\dfrac{e}{f} = \dfrac{c}{d}$, then $\dfrac{a}{b} = \dfrac{e}{f}$.

Lacking this sign, and lacking also the ability to conceive of ratios as algebraic entities or even as numerical quantities, the mathematician of antiquity was obliged to make a detour by way of equimultiples. As presented in Euclid, however, Eudoxus' proof resembles less a mathematical operation than a sequence of syllogisms. For, after all, it is a matter of proving a truth belonging more to logic than to mathematics: if A is B and if C is B, then A is C. If we simply quote Euclid's last sentences, and interpolate the reference to definition IV, we shall see that his final argument reduces to a so-called syllogism in *Disamis*:

> If *ma* is greater than, equal to or less than *nb*, *me* is correspondingly greater than, equal to or less than *nf*. And *ma* and *me* are equimultiples of *a* and *e*, while *nc* and *nf* are equimultiples of *c* and *f*.
>
> Now, by definition, the ratios between the magnitudes taken two at a time are identical when the equimultiples of the first and the third are simultaneously greater than, equal to or less than the equimultiples of the second and the fourth.
>
> Therefore *a* is to *b* in the same ratio as *e* is to *f*.

On this account Eudoxus deserves to be considered as the founder of the syllogism, of which Aristotle was to establish the formal theory only fifteen years later.

> 7. If any number of magnitudes be proportional, as one of the antecedents is to one of the consequents, so will all the antecedents be to all consequents. (*Elem.* V, Prop. 12, Arist. *Eth. Nicom.* 1131ᵇ13)

The statement is deficient, in that it does not specify that the antecedent magnitude and the consequent magnitude must be those of some one of the proportional ratios, and not just any of the antecedent magnitudes and any of the consequent magnitudes. In other words, one has to consider the sum of the numerators and the sum of the denominators of several ordinary fractions which are proportional to one another and prove that these sums are proportional to any of these fractions whatever. In quoting this theorem of Theudius or Eudoxus, Aristotle expresses it more happily:

The whole is to the whole what each part is to each part respectively. (*Eth. Nicom.* 1131^{b}13)

Let $\frac{a}{b} = \frac{c}{d} = \frac{e}{f}$ etc., it is asserted that $\frac{a+c+e+..}{b+d+f+..} = \frac{a}{b}$

The theorem is proved by comparing the multiples *ma* and *nb* with the equimultiples $m(a+c+e...)$ and $n(b+d+f+...)$

8. If a first magnitude have to a second the same ratio as a third has to a fourth, and the first be greater than the third, the second will also be greater than the fourth; if equal, equal; and if less, less. (*Elem.* V, Prop. 14, Arist. *Meteor.* 376^{a}11)

Let $\frac{a}{b} = \frac{c}{d}$; it is asserted that, if $a > = < c$, then $b > = < d$.

The theorem is proved by starting from theorems 4 and 5, and taking in successions $a > c$, then $a = c$, and finally $a < c$. Let us take example $a > c$:

By theorem 4, $\qquad \frac{a}{b} > \frac{c}{b}$ $\quad$ or $\quad$ $\frac{c}{b} < \frac{a}{b}$

therefore $\qquad \frac{c}{b} < \frac{c}{d}$

from which, by theorem 5, it can be concluded that $b > d$.

Similarly in succession for $a = c$ and for $a < c$.

$\qquad\qquad\qquad\qquad\qquad\qquad\qquad$ Q.E.D.

After this series of theorems, all the necessary elements are in position for the demonstration of the famous theorem on the transformation of proportions:

9. If four magnitudes be proportional, they will also be proportional alternately. (*Elem.* V, Prop. 16, Arist. *Anal. Post.* 74^{a}17 and *Meteor.* 376^{a}11)

Let $\dfrac{a}{b} = \dfrac{c}{d}$; it is asserted that $\dfrac{a}{c} = \dfrac{b}{d}$

The theorem is proved by starting from theorems 7 and 8;

If
$$\frac{a}{b} = \frac{c}{b}$$

then on the one hand $\dfrac{ma}{mb} = \dfrac{a}{b}$, on the other $\dfrac{nc}{nd} = \dfrac{c}{d}$

So, by theorem 6, $\quad \dfrac{ma}{mb} = \dfrac{c}{d} \quad$ and $\quad \dfrac{nc}{nd} = \dfrac{ma}{mb}$

But if ma is greater than, equal to or less than nc, mb will be correspondingly greater than, equal to or less than nd. Therefore the ratios between ma and nc on the one hand, mb and nd on the other, are identical. And what is true of equimultiples is also true of the non-multiplied magnitudes. Therefore:

$$\frac{a}{c} = \frac{b}{d}$$

Q.E.D.

The reader who has had the patience and (let us hope) the pleasure of following the rigorous sequence of theorems and proofs up to this point will not fail to appreciate its abstract character. If, as its author intended, this theory still forms part of geometry, this must now be geometry without figures. But one must feel that it is a mistake to continue calling by the name of geometry a science of relations going entirely beyond shapes, just as it goes beyond numbers. At first glance, one might be tempted to say that Eudoxus was moving in the immaterial world of the Platonic ideas, and that he was practising on those primary beings that 'science superior to mathematics' which Plato advocated under the name of dialectic. But this explanation cannot satisfy us, for it is obvious that Eudoxus's 'magnitudes' are not the same as Plato's 'ideas'.

In point of fact, an unbridgeable gulf divides these two

conceptions. Preoccupied entirely with the problem of the knowledge of being, whatever efforts he might make to strip all material appearance from the imaginary archetypes of the entities he subjects to his analysis, and to rid them of all substance, and although he might eventually succeed in reducing them, not indeed to a number, but to the principle of Number—that is, Unity—the disciple of Plato must still regard them as real beings. For Eudoxus it was quite otherwise: the magnitudes whose ratios he described and catalogued never presented themselves to him as real beings. If we have to find a suitable expression for them in our own language, the phrase 'algebraic term' would suit them best. As a matter of fact, *magnitudes* have this in common with algebra, that they reduce the objects of the different mathematical sciences to their simplest and most general form. But they have the additional virtue of withdrawing all their importance from mathematical objects as such, and of concentrating all the elements of reasoning on to mathematical relations alone. If the last theorem quoted merely had the effect of enabling the mathematician to determine some of the unknowns in a system of equations, for example in astronomy, one could at a pinch maintain that Eudoxus' algebra postulates numerical or geometrical realities. But this would be to misunderstand the true nature of the theory of proportion, which is neither more nor less than an admirable chapter in mathematical logic. As such, it is diametrically opposed to Platonic dialectic and points straight to Aristotle's logic.

The theorems which follow the one on transformed proportion do not present the same interest, but they typify the fertility characteristic of axiomatic mathematics, whose task is to exhaust all the truths latent in the original definitions. Of the eight theorems which, in Euclid, follow my last theorem and still belong to Eudoxus' theory, taken together with two others of later date, there is not one which reveals a new relation, while several of the first theorems, for example those numbered 4 and 5 in my list, only make explicit the immediate implications of the definitions and can be described as preliminary lemmas. In order not to make this chapter too long, four only need be quoted, chosen for their special interest.

10. If magnitudes be proportional *componendo*, they will also be proportional *separando*. (*Elem.* V, Prop. 17)

Algebraically: if $\dfrac{a}{b} = \dfrac{c}{d}$ then $\dfrac{a-b}{b} = \dfrac{c-d}{d}$

11. If magnitudes be proportional *separando*, they will also be proportional *componendo*. (*Elem.* V, Prop. 18)

Algebraically: if $\dfrac{a}{b} = \dfrac{c}{d}$ then $\dfrac{a+b}{b} = \dfrac{c+d}{d}$

12. If, as a whole is to a whole, so is a part subtracted to a part subtracted, the remainder will also be to the remainder as whole to whole. (*Elem.* V, Prop. 19)

Algebraically: if $\dfrac{a}{b} = \dfrac{c}{d}$ then $\dfrac{a-c}{b-d} = \dfrac{a}{b}$

13. If a first magnitude have to a second the same ratio as a third has to a fourth, and also a fifth have to the second the same ratio as a sixth to the fourth, the first and fifth added together will have to the second the same ratio as the third and sixth have to the fourth. (*Elem.* V, Prop. 24, Arist. *Meteor.* 376ª22)

Algebraically: if $\dfrac{a}{c} = \dfrac{d}{f}$ and $\dfrac{b}{c} = \dfrac{e}{f}$

then $\dfrac{a+b}{c} = \dfrac{d+e}{f}$

It is easy to see that the conclusion relies on theorem 11, about added magnitudes. But the proof also brings in a theorem which, expressed algebraically, would read as follows (*Elem.* V, Prop. 22):

If $\dfrac{a}{b} = \dfrac{d}{e}$ and $\dfrac{b}{c} = \dfrac{e}{f}$ then $\dfrac{a}{c} = \dfrac{d}{f}$

This intermediate theorem allows one to extract from theorem 13 the equality

$$\frac{a}{b} = \frac{d}{e}$$

from which by a repeated application of the same intermediate theorem one can conclude that

$$\frac{a + b}{c} = \frac{d + e}{f}$$

Q.E.D.

Such, in broad outline, is the general theory of proportion, one of the most remarkable contributions made by ancient mathematics to the progress of human thought.

The golden section

After having quoted the theorems on proportion, Eudemus makes mention in a single sentence of Eudoxus' work on the golden section, and of his application in this work of the method of analysis, and also alludes to the influence of Plato. What is this all about?

At the beginning of Book XIII of Euclid's *Elements*, which covers the construction of the regular solids, the ancient editors added, in the guise of a preface, five theorems on the section in extreme and mean ratio known today as the golden section. This section, or proportion, has its origin in the following geometrical problem: given a segment of a straight line, to divide it into two segments such that the smaller is to the greater in the same ratio as the greater is to the given straight-line segment, that is to say, to the sum of the smaller and the greater segments. Algebraically:

$$\frac{a}{b} = \frac{b}{a + b}$$

This three-termed proportion is a special case of the geometric mean, but it is by no means certain that Eudoxus handled it along with the other means. On the contrary, everything suggests that this interest in it was connected with those problems in which the method of analysis was most often used—the constructions of the regular solids.

Before Eudoxus, the golden section had already caught the interest of many mathematicians. Theaetetus, in particular, had been obliged to use it in constructing the dodecahedron and the icosahedron. In the first collection of *Elements* to contain a chapter on the regular solids (by Leodamas of Thasos or Leon), some theorems on the section had been necessary as an introduction to the constructions of pentagonal figures. Now we know that Leodamas was the first to have applied the method known as 'analysis' in geometrical proofs and, as in the case of Eudoxus and the golden section, tradition has it that he learned it from Plato. In the generation after Eudoxus, this method was applied more extensively but never far from its point of departure in the problems of spatial geometry. In this context, it acquired a reputation of being the only method whose success was guaranteed. It is not surprising, then, if the first theorems of Euclid's Book XIII still have the threefold characteristic of paving a way for the construction of the solids, of providing the sole treatment of the golden section, and of being presented not only with a proof by the standard methods, but also with a second proof using the method of analysis.

Let us pause for a moment to look at this method before going back to the golden section. When it is applied to the solution of a problem, analysis consists in taking the resolved problem as one's starting-point and studying the implications of the solution, so working back to the statement of the problem. In the proof of a theorem, the mathematician proceeds similarly. He first considers the theorem as proved, then analyses the implications of this conclusion, so working his way back until he reaches a proposition already established. In both cases the method is regressive, and its name of 'analysis' is clearly explained by its procedure, since it breaks down a complex truth into its constituent parts. As Aristotle judiciously remarks,

> The last step in the analysis is the first in the order of becoming. (*Eth. Nicom.* 1112^{b}23)

Inasmuch as it goes from complex to simple, from whole to element, analysis is vaguely reminiscent of Plato's 'ascending dialectic', by which an object progressively loses its material aspects, until its true essence is revealed. It also recalls, more closely, the method of dichotomy or diaeresis, which consists in reducing every composite being, after a series of divisions, to its elementary units. Developed by Plato himself and applied by him to mathematical ideas above all, this latter method has left its mark on his work and on that of his disciples; there is a suggestion of it, for example, in Speusippus' analysis of the number 10. But this resemblance remains superficial. The mathematicians are as far distant from Plato as things are from axioms. When, in the *Timaeus*, Plato breaks down all the objects in Nature into five elements having the forms of polyhedra, and then each polyhedron into polygonal faces, and finally each face into right-angled triangles, he discovers at the end of his analysis not a primitive truth capable of proving the truth of his initial object, but a new object which proves nothing at all about the other. The mathematician, on the other hand, comes back by analysis to an already established proposition, whether this be a proved theorem, a definition or an axiom, and this certainty is sought for only as a way of guaranteeing the truth of the new, and initially precarious, assertion subjected to this verification. The mathematician's established propositions are linked together by a tight network of logical relations—and mathematics is the science of these relations. The objects identified in succession by Platonic dialectic or by the method of diaeresis which derives from it may be linked by a physical connection, such as that established by modern chemistry between an atom and a molecule, but there is no logical connection between them. So there is an essential difference between the methods of analysis as practised by Plato and by the mathematicians, and the filiation which Eudemus believed to be discernible between them—for the remark about Leodamas is as much due to him as that about Eudoxus—does not survive an examination of their respective principles.

Let us go back to the golden section. The five theorems with which Book XIII of the *Elements* opens are given proofs of the standard type. But in the majority of our manuscripts each of the proofs is duplicated by another proof, itself in two parts entitled 'analysis' and 'synthesis'. Although the variations shown by the manuscript tradition in the placing of these supplementary proofs very probably mark them as an interpolation, there is more reason to believe that they date back to the mathematicians of the Academy, in broad outline at least, than to attribute them to a later commentator. In any case they illustrate the methods adopted by Euclid's predecessors in dealing with this topic, and this indeed is their sole interest. However, it is unlikely that the five theorems, with their five proofs by analysis, come from Eudoxus alone. The first four, in fact, establish the properties of the golden section by means of theorems taken exclusively from the traditional geometry of figures, the geometry of Hippocrates of Chios and the first books of Euclid. These might date back through Leon's *Elements*, as far as Leodamas of Thasos. But the fifth has quite a different character. Not only is it far less useful in the construction of polyhedra—it is called on for this purpose only once in the whole of Book XIII—but also its proof by analysis is based entirely on the general theory of proportion, which is the work of Eudoxus. For this reason it is included here as a vestige of his work on the golden section, with all the reservations about its authenticity which its—undoubtedly abnormal—manuscript transmission demands.

Here is the theorem in question, as set out by Euclid:

If a straight line be cut in extreme and mean ratio, and there be added to it a straight line equal to the greater segment, the whole straight line has been cut in extreme and mean ratio, and the original straight line is the greater segment. (*Elem.* XIII, Prop. 5)

$$\overset{\textstyle a'}{\underset{\textstyle}{|\cdots\cdots|}}\overset{\textstyle a}{\underset{\textstyle}{\rule{2cm}{0.4pt}}}\overset{\textstyle b}{\underset{\textstyle}{\rule{1cm}{0.4pt}|}}$$

Let the straight line $a+b$ be divided in extreme and mean ratio, let a be the greater segment and let

$a'=a$: it is then asserted that $\dfrac{a'+a+b}{a+b} = \dfrac{a+b}{a'}$

and that $a+b$ is the greater segment.

Since $a'+a+b$ have been divided in extreme and mean ratio and $a+b$ is the greater segment, then

$$\frac{a'+a+b}{a+b} = \frac{a+b}{a'}$$

Now, by hypothesis, $\quad a' = a$

therefore $\qquad \dfrac{a' + a + b}{a + b} = \dfrac{a + b}{a}$

If we apply theorem 12 of the theory of proportion,

$$\frac{a' + a + b}{a'} = \frac{a + b}{b}$$

But the straight lines represented by the numerators are added straight lines, therefore, by virtue of theorem 10 of the theory of proportion,

$$\frac{a + b}{a'} = \frac{a}{b}$$

Now, by hypothesis, $\quad a' = a$

therefore $\qquad \dfrac{a + b}{a} = \dfrac{a}{b}$

And this statement is true since $a + b$ has been divided in extreme and mean ratio.

This demonstration cannot be followed by the standard 'Q.E.D.' In contrast to the position in proofs carried out 'by synthesis', it is actually not the last statement which has to be proved, but the first. Everything proceeds as if the mathematician had first conceived a new theorem by intuition, and then attempted to connect it back to theorems already known or, as in this case, to argue back to the given conditions. The ancient commentators realized, in addition, that analysis had the merit of showing whether or not a theorem is capable of proof: when the theorem cannot be reduced to any previously accepted truth, this indicates that it is un-provable. Thus it appears that the analytical method, far from slowing up the advance of mathematics by its regressive procedure, on the contrary encouraged imaginative boldness. At a period when neither arithmetic nor geometry had yet produced a sufficient number of theorems to provide a mathematician faced with any new problem with a selection of truths capable of suggesting a solution, it was simpler to consider the problem as solved and then to seek a solution by working back to the original hypothesis. One must also conclude that the method of analysis had been developed at a stage when geometrical theorems were still being presented with proofs which were scarcely standardized, since Eudemus asserts that the order and method of arrangement of the Elements are the work of Leodamas, Theaetetus and Archytas: faced with anarchy, it was tempting for a mathematician to perfect a method which was applicable in principle to the whole of geometry.

In short, proof by analysis was the most promising instrument in a particularly intuitive field of research, and this leads us back to Plato by a road quite different from that envisaged by Eudemus. It leads to him because all Plato's philosophical speculation is intuitive in its approach; because his thought was continually probing the universe by sheer sympathy; because his very dialectic takes as its starting-point not established truths or working hypotheses, as in a mathematician's reasoning, but visions and myths. True, neither Plato nor his disciples had yet marked off what we call intuitive knowledge by a name or a definition. But in the attitude of the philosophers of the Academy towards metaphysical problems this form of penetration was nevertheless predominant. So it is natural that the mathematicians who moved in their field of influence should have exploited in their own research an intellectual approach giving immediate access to truths which were at once the most remote and, apparently, the hardest to prove. Analysis provides mathematical intuition with a secure defence against illusion. It forces the mathematician who has initially jumped too far ahead to retrace his steps, and compels him to measure the intervening distance. It thus belongs to the arsenal of devices brought into use between 370 and 350 in order to transform the edifice of mathematics into an impregnable fortress. As a method of controlling intuition, its standing is the same as that of Leon's *diorismos*, which served, if later reports are to be believed, to determine on what conditions a given problem allows of one or several solutions or, on the other hand, of no solution at all. And indeed, analysis may well show the necessity for a *diorismos* by indicating, in the final stage of its reasoning, that the problem in question admits of a solution only on certain conditions.

Proportional volumes

As explained earlier, we do not know what application Eudoxus had in mind when he formulated his general theory of proportion, supposing that he did not develop it simply for its own sake. In his theorem on the golden section we encountered one vestige of a more extended piece of work whose final aim also escapes us. We know that his research in astronomy made it indispensable. Now, in conclusion, we shall see what effect it had in some theorems about certain proportional volumes, which could also have found an application in astronomical calculations. None of these applications, however, appears by itself to justify the elaboration of this theory, and we are accordingly forced merely to acknowledge its existence and its uses without pinpointing its origin. The theorems on proportional volumes themselves also come to us out of their original context, and perhaps represent fragments of a theory developed elsewhere than in a treatise on geometry. In short, all we can do today is consider them for what they are, and we must give up the hope of incorporating them into a wider programme of research. Their only visible link is with the theory of proportion, and we shall have to concentrate on that.

It is not easy to extricate these theorems from the testimonies about them, since they originated, as we shall see, largely in unknown circumstances. The most convenient starting-point is a historical report which Archimedes repeated, in more or less the same terms, in the introductions to three of his treatises on geometry. What follows is the full statement obtained by a comparison of the three versions:

> Of unequal lines, unequal surfaces, or unequal solids, the greater exceeds the less by such a magnitude as is capable, if added continually to itself, of exceeding any magnitude of those which are comparable with one another. The earlier geometers have also used this lemma, for it is by the use of this lemma that they have proved the propositions:

1. That circles are to one another in the duplicate ratio of their diameters; (=Eucl. *Elem.* XII, Prop. 2)

2. That spheres are to one another in the triplicate ratio of their diameters. (=Eucl. *Elem.* XII, Prop. 18)

And they proved further by assuming a certain lemma similar to that aforesaid:

3. That every pyramid is one third part of the prism which has the same base with the pyramid and equal height; (=Eucl. *Elem.* XII, Prop. 7 coroll.)

4. Also that every cone is one third part of the cylinder having the same base with the cone and equal height. (*Quadrat. Parab.* p. 264 and *De Sphaera et Cylindro* p. 4 =Eucl. *Elem.* XII, Prop. 10)

Two versions of this report specify that theorems 3 and 4 were proved for the first time by Eudoxus, whilst Democritus, without being able to state a proof, had already formulated theorem 3. One ancient commentator also attributes theorem 1 to Eudoxus, and Hero the mathematician maintains that no one before him could have proved this theorem, any more than theorem 4. So the witnesses from antiquity combine to emphasize the importance of the proposition quoted by Archimedes, without which three of these theorems (the first, the third and the fourth) would have remained unproved even where already known. Hero further implies that the author of his proposition was Eudoxus.

The proposition quoted by Archimedes, and known to modern historians by the unfortunate name of 'the lemma of Archimedes', manifestly dates from a time before any general theory of proportion existed. It was nevertheless associated with a theory of proportion whose transitional character has already been shown above (p. 49). The evidence of Archimedes and Hero suggests that it was formulated in order to extend the application of this theory to volumes, and probably to surfaces also, while the older procedure of *anthyphairesis*, worked out for numbers, could be used strictly only when comparing sets of lines. Before Eudoxus, then, geometers had tried to group the proportionalities of circular figures, using as intermediary a general definition of ratio. Or perhaps this was after Eudoxus, if Hero's statement means that we owe to him not only the proof of these theorems, but also the formulation of the proposition which made the proof possible. This minor difference will be clarified later.

The four theorems quoted by Archimedes are also preserved by Euclid. Together with some preliminary theorems, they provide the framework for Book XII of the *Elements*. So one would expect to find frequent references to 'the lemma of Archimedes'. But this is not so at all. Wherever it should appear, Euclid goes back to the following proposition:

> Two unequal magnitudes being set out, if from the greater there be subtracted a magnitude greater than its half, and from that which is left a magnitude greater than its half, and if this process be repeated continually, there will be left some magnitude which will be less than the lesser magnitude set out. (*Elem.* X, Prop. 1)

This proposition comes from Book X, in which it helps, directly or indirectly, to prove several theorems. As this Book is devoted to a subject-matter dealt with by Theaetetus, there are several reasons for thinking that the introductory proposition is taken from him also. That is the reason why the name of 'the lemma of Theaetetus' has been suggested for it. Euclid's proof, however, makes use of definition II of Eudoxus' general theory of proportion and cannot therefore date back to Theaetetus. Furthermore, in the wording of this lemma, there figures the term 'magnitude' which, used in this sense, is characteristic of the same theory of Eudoxus. So the demonstrations in Book XII lead neither to a 'lemma of Archimedes', nor to a 'lemma of Theaetetus', but to a proposition which no one before Eudoxus could apparently have formulated in these terms.

The situation is consequently clearer, in spite of the apparent contradiction between Archimedes and Euclid: the lemma which made it possible to prove the theorems on the proportionalities of circular figures was recast in the course of its history. One may suppose that the first mathematician to treat the proportions of volumes systematically —Leodamas, or Leon, for instance—had successively stated and proved:

(1) the lemma on added magnitudes quoted by Archimedes and known by the name of 'the lemma of Archimedes';

(2) an inverse lemma on subtracted magnitudes, now lost, representing the prototype of the proposition in Euclid Book X known as 'the lemma of Theaetetus';

(3) the first two theorems in Archimedes' list, relating to the proportionalities of circles and spheres, and attributed by Archimedes only to 'earlier geometers'.

Taking up the theory again a little later, Eudoxus must have been guided by his own work to base it no longer on 'the lemma of Archimedes', but on the more general statement formulated in definition II of his theory of proportion. From this statement, he derived the so-called 'lemma of Theaetetus' in the form reproduced by Euclid, and based on this lemma the four theorems listed by Archimedes, together with the four proofs which accompany them in Book XII of Euclid. Archimedes' allusion to a certain lemma 'similar to that aforesaid' could then refer to the recasting which transformed lemma 2 of the above theory into one identical with that in Euclid. In this indirect way these four theorems thus connected up with the general theory of proportion.

The proofs proposed by Eudoxus are too long for all of them to be quoted here, even in a shortened form. Let us therefore confine ourselves to the proof of the theorem about circles proportional to the squares on their radii, which may be selected for two reasons: firstly, on account of its probable connection with the theory of the celestial spheres, and secondly to illustrate the method of proof known as 'exhaustion', which Eudoxus invented for the comparison of circular figures. Let us first recall its terms:

Circles are to one another in the duplicate ratio of their diameters. (Eucl. *Elem.* XII, Prop. 2)

Let us suppose that the circle *ABCD* is not in the same ratio to the circle *EFGH* as the squares on their respective diameters, BD^2 and FH^2; one must then allow that it stands in this relation to an area *s* smaller or greater than this circle (rule of the fourth proportional).

Suppose, first, that *s* is smaller than the circle *EFGH*.

Let us begin by inscribing the square *EFGH* in the circle *EFGH* and likewise circumscribe a square round this circle: the circumscribed square has an area double that of the inscribed square, since its side is equal to the diagonal of the latter ($FH^2 = FE^2 + EH^2$), and it is larger than half the circle since the circumscribed square is larger than the circle.

Now let us draw triangles *EKF, FLG, GMH* and *HNE* in the arcs marked off by the vertices of the inscribed square; each one of these is larger than one-half the segments of the circle *EKF, FLG*, etc., since they are each equal to one-half of the rectangles *EKF, FLG*, etc., enclosing these segments.

Let us once again bisect the arcs marked off by the vertices of these triangles, and describe new triangles in the new arcs. Repeat the same operation as many times as necessary (but not until 'exhaustion'—this term is entirely incorrect): at a certain point, the remaining segments will together constitute, in virtue of the lemma known as 'the lemma of Theaetetus' (in reality 'the lemma of Eudoxus') an area smaller than that by which the circle *EFGH* exceeds the area *s*. At this point also, the inscribed polygon—as it might be, the octagon *EKFLGMHN*—will become larger than the area *s*, since the sum of the segments represents the difference between the area of the circle and that of the polygon.

Let us inscribe a similar polygon *AOBPCQDR* in the first circle; the squares on the diameters BD^2 and FH^2 are to one another as corresponding polygons. So the first circle should be to the area *s* as the polygon inscribed in this circle is to the other polygon. If we call the first circle *a*, its polygon *o* and the other polygon *u*, then it should follow that:

$$\frac{a}{s} = \frac{o}{u}$$

and after exchanging terms (theorem 9)

$$\frac{a}{o} = \frac{s}{u}$$

But the first circle (a) is by definition larger than the inscribed polygon (o), and the area s, as a result of the procedure described, was found to be smaller than the other polygon (u). There is therefore a contradiction, and the squares BD^2 and FH^2 are not proportional to the areas a and s. And what is true of the circle $ABCD$ (a) as compared with s will be true by an identical argument of the circle $EFGH$ as compared with an area smaller than the circle $ABCD$.

Let us now suppose that s is larger than the circle $EFGH$, which we shall call e. By virtue of the original supposition:

$$\frac{FH^2}{BD^2} = \frac{s}{a}$$

Considering also an area t smaller than the circle a, and such that

$$\frac{s}{a} = \frac{e}{t}$$

we shall then also have

$$\frac{FH^2}{BD^2} = \frac{e}{t}$$

But it has already been proved that the squares FH^2 and BD^2 cannot be to one another as the circle $EFGH$ (e) to an area smaller than the circle $ABCD$. There is therefore once again a contradiction.

Now, if the squares on the diameters considered do not bear the same ratio to one another that one of the circles does to an area either smaller or greater than the area of the other circle, they must be in the same ratio as one of the circles to the other circle. Q.E.D.

Taking this first demonstration as a starting-point, the second theorem, concerning spheres, can be proved easily: replace the squares by cubes, the polygons by polyhedra and the supposed areas by any chosen volumes. The theorem relating the cylinder to the cone, the fourth as listed by Archimedes, is likewise proved by an exhaustion procedure applied to a hypothetical solid. Eudoxus had previously established, again by the same procedure, that every prism

is to the pyramid having the same base and height as itself
in the ratio of the cubes on their corresponding sides. Elsewhere he had established, this time merely from an analysis
of the triangles, that a triangular-based prism can be split up
into three equal pyramids having the same base and the
same height as the original prism. These two propositions
combined together gave the third theorem in Archimedes'
list. So we find, in the working out of each of the four
theorems, the lemma appearing at the beginning of Book X
of the *Elements*—what may be called 'the lemma of Eudoxus';
and equally, we find the application of the method of exhaustion connected up with this lemma.

The Delos problem

From evidence which is in other respects rather obscure—
though definite at least on this point—it appears that
Eudoxus also applied the theory of proportion to the solution
of what was called 'the Delos problem'. Practically all the
information left to us by antiquity about the different attacks
on this problem comes by way of Eudemus of Rhodes, who
is a reliable source. As regards Eudoxus, however, our information comes only from a popular work inspired by
Eudemus, the dialogue *Platonicus* written about 240 by
Eratosthenes. Certainly, Eratosthenes was one of the greatest
scientists of ancient times and his authority ensures the
accuracy of his evidence in matters of mathematics, but he
is also a court writer and the choice of dialogue form, in the
case we are considering, indicates his intention to give
literary elegance priority over historical exactitude.

Having come to Athens from distant Cyrenaica around
260 B.C., Eratosthenes had there attended the famous schools
which at that time were attracting the intellectual élite of the
whole Greek world, and he had heard the greatest philosophers expounding their doctrines: Zeno the Stoic, Arcesilas at the Academy, Apelles and Bion among the Cynics.
He was throughout drawn by preference towards the
Academy, where the packed audiences brought to his
mind the time when, in the very same place, a brilliant group
of disciples pressed around Plato. Called to Egypt to the

court of Ptolemy Euergetes around 240, he presented himself as a pupil of Arcesilas, then still head of the Academy, and it was to the memory of Plato that he intended to dedicate the work which we must now consider, one of the first that he wrote for the public of Alexandria.

The dialogue *Platonicus* carried the reader back to the year 368 and placed him in the Academy as an onlooker at a conversation between the most celebrated geometers of the day under the leadership of Plato. The philosopher began by telling how a deputation of inhabitants of Delos had come to him some time before to ask his help in solving a serious problem. As an epidemic of plague was ravaging their island the Delians had consulted the oracle of Apollo, and the God had commanded them through him to double the size of his chief altar, which was cubical in shape. They had accordingly placed on top of this cube a second cube of identical dimensions. But the plague had not ceased: the oracle accused them of not having obeyed Apollo's order. They then decided to enlist the help of the most distinguished philosopher in Greece and a deputation had been sent to Plato. In Plato's view the accusation of disobedience could mean only one thing, that the god was reproaching the Delians for having neglected geometry. He then showed them how, for the geometer, the problem of doubling a cube reduced to the following problem: to construct two mean proportionals between two given straight-line segments.

Given two unequal squares a^2 and b^2, the area which will be the mean proportional between them is that of the rectangle ab, called the *medial* rectangle, produced by multiplying the side of the first square by that of the second, or *vice versa*:

$$\frac{a^2}{ab} = \frac{ab}{b^2}$$

But if two unequal cubes a^3 and b^3 are considered, multiplying the base of the first by the side of the second, and *vice versa*, that is to say the base of the second by the side of the first (on the analogy of the former calculation), results in not one, but two mean volumes, having the form of rectangular parallelepipeds;

a^2b and ab^2. These parallelepipeds are the mean proportionals between a^3 and b^3:

$$\frac{a^3}{a^2b} = \frac{a^2b}{ab^2} = \frac{ab^2}{b^3}$$

If we replace the four volumes represented by these
expressions by the successive magnitudes $a, x, y,$ and b,
it appears that the problem of the duplication of the
cube reduces, in geometrical terms, to the construction
of two magnitudes x and y as mean proportionals between two given magnitudes a and b such that $b = 2a$.

Eratosthenes put this new formulation of the problem
into the mouth of Plato, who indeed quotes it in the *Timaeus*
(32 AB), but as an assiduous reader of Eudemus he was well
aware that it had already been put forward by Hippocrates
of Chios. At this point in his story, the philosopher in his
turn had to confess his embarrassment and ask the geometers
for the answer which the Delian deputation was seeking.
He accordingly invited them to consider this famous problem
themselves. Let us not deceive ourselves about the authenticity of this setting: while it may be true that the solutions
Eratosthenes reported, using this expedient, were set out by
the geometers whom he names, it is on the other hand quite
evident that their meeting in Athens, the date of 368 (chosen
in order to synchronize their works—it survived in the
ancient tradition as the date of Eudoxus[1]) and the stimulus
of Plato are none of them more than literary fictions.

The two most prominent of Plato's guests are Archytas
and Eudoxus. But they are accompanied by their pupils,
whom Plato invites to speak first of all. With great ingenuity, they put forward mechanical solutions involving
apparatus equipped with grooves or engraved curves,
called *mesographs*, enabling one to determine the values of
the required means for any values whatever of the corresponding extreme magnitudes. Plato himself is not above
joining in their game and puts forward a still more ingenious
machine for their consideration. But he soon calls a halt to
this misguided line of research, as being unworthy of a true
geometer, and admonishes them firmly:

1. See above, p. 86, footnote.

You want to find these means without recourse to logical argument and you thereby condemn and destroy the proper virtue of geometry, bringing this science down to the level of tangible objects instead of raising it to the knowledge of immaterial and eternal ideas over which rules the god who is—through them—eternally god. (After Plutarch, *Quaest. conviv.* VIII, 2, 1.)

Silenced by this severe reprimand, the pupils of Archytas and Eudoxus then leave their respective masters to put their views. Archytas speaks first. Taking as his starting-point one of the supposed mechanical solutions, he sets himself to translate it into geometrical figures and provides a proof of the greatest interest which, most fortunately, has been preserved for us in its entirety by Eudemus. Let it merely be said here, without going into more detail, that Archytas determined the required means by starting from a point situated at the intersection of a cylinder, a cone and a semi-circle. The figure below shows the cylinder upright, the

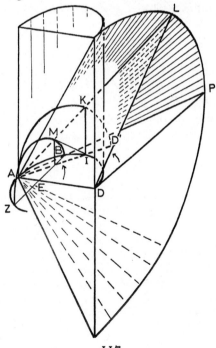

cone formed by rotating the right-angled triangle *PDA* (alternative position in *LDA*) round its vertical *DA* (coincident with a diameter of the cylinder) and the movable semi-circle *AKD'* pivoting horizontally round the vertical at point *A*. The semi-circle *BZE* is the curve described on the surface of the cylinder by the point *M* carried round by the rotation of the triangle generating the cone. The given straight-line segments, between which the two mean proportionals are to be constructed, are the segments *AB* and *AD*, which form respectively a chord and a diameter of the base of the cylinder. The required mean proportionals are the segments *KA* and *KI*.

In one sense Archytas kept to the rules of geometry, since the solids he employed are made up of circles and straight lines. But the representation of these solids by a perspective drawing implied a projection on to a plane for which ruler and compass are not sufficient. His solution therefore remained a theoretical one, inspired as it was by mechanisms which set in motion plane figures fixed to axes. However, it conformed with the oldest conception of circular volumes, which were represented as it were from inside—as a hole cut out of a mass by the revolution of a surface around an axis—from which originated the Pythagorean idea of the generation of solids by planes.

After Archytas' solution, Eratosthenes quoted that of Eudoxus. Unfortunately, owing to an accident in the transmission of the texts, it is not extant today. In the sixth century A.D., indeed, the mathematician Eutocius, having a version in front of him, writes as follows:

As to the solution of Eudoxus of Cnidus, we have abstained from transcribing it because, after saying in his introduction that he discovered it by means of curved lines, he not only makes no use of curved lines in his proof, but furthermore he treats a discrete proportion which he had discovered as a continuous proportion, which is unthinkable of a mathematician such as Eudoxus, and even, I dare say, of any man with the slightest knowledge of geometry. (*Comm. in Archimed.* p. 56)

What can have led Eutocius to brush aside his informant's text with such severity? One might at first suppose that he did not understand Eudoxus' solution. Indeed, is it not striking that he could not even explain the apparent disagreement between the introduction and the proof? Eudoxus might well have discovered a way of solving the problem using curves which were impossible to construct with legitimate geometrical instruments, and then set out to express these curves by means of proportions. As to the alleged confusion between continuous proportions—of the type $\frac{a}{b} = \frac{b}{c}$ and discrete proportions—of the type $\frac{a}{b} = \frac{c}{d}$ —this could be due to a lack of attention on Eutocius' part in studying Eudoxus' argument, which was undoubtedly a difficult one. Still, we must take into account also the possibility of a defective text, or else of an abridgement which had become incomprehensible on account of its conciseness.

Despite his deliberate silence, we learn two important facts from Eutocius: Eudoxus' solution was based on the study of certain curves and it introduced the theory of proportion. The first is corroborated by Eratosthenes, who in an epigram dedicated to King Ptolemy refers in passing to

'the curved form of lines as is described by the god-fearing Eudoxus.'

The second is also supported by Eratosthenes, though indirectly, inasmuch as his dialogue contained an important account of the distinction between continuous proportions and discrete proportions. These two indications do not make it possible to reconstruct the lost solution. But they do mark off the branch of geometry in which we must look for it, establishing that it is that of analytical geometry. One may, indeed, consider that the proportion which he studied was a fixed relation between variable magnitudes and that the curves leading him to this proportion were the locus of this relation. Curves appear again in Menaechmus' solution, which involves a parabola and a hyperbola. As for the notion of a geometrical locus which is indispensable for all analytical geometry, even at the embryonic stage which Eudoxus could not have surpassed, it appears quite clearly in a theorem which Aristotle probably takes from the *Elements* of Theudius of Magnesia or from some work of the same period:

> Given two points in a plane and a ratio between unequal straight lines, it is possible to describe a circle in the plane such that the straight lines inflected from the given points to the circumference of the circle shall have a ratio the same as the given one. (*Meteor.* 375^b 25–376^a 9 *passim*)[1]

The term 'geometrical locus' does not yet seem to be known to Aristotle, and this is perhaps a sign that the notion it expresses had not yet been isolated from neighbouring ideas. However, the author of the theorem has grasped it quite satisfactorily, without the help of a co-ordinate system and without yet possessing any definition of the circle as the locus made up of points satisfying certain conditions. It is interesting, too, that he approaches this idea from the theory of proportion, making tacit use here of theorem 3 (see p. 94). With a little daring, but without being rash, one may be tempted to conclude that the geometrical locus is yet another of the numerous offspring of this theory.

The third solution reported by Eratosthenes is that of Menaechmus, who figured in the dialogue, sometimes as a pupil of Eudoxus, sometimes as a first-class mathematician in his own right. His name is connected in antiquity with the 'triad of Menaechmus', namely the identification of the three curves, other than the circle, which can be determined by the intersection of a plane with a cone: the ellipse, the parabola and the hyperbola. The name 'solid loci', which was applied to these curves from the fourth century on, indicates well how they were conceived and how Menaechmus had defined them—though without yet resorting to this term himself. Although they had originally been identified on the cone, and for this reason had also gone by the

1. This theorem is mentioned again in the third century only by Apollonius of Perga, who certainly did not take it from Aristotle. This parallel between the two authors indicates a common older source.

name of 'conic sections', they certainly no longer signified for Menaechmus, as for Archytas, the mobile intersection of a surface with a figure of revolution. He is no longer interested in anything but the properties of the cone and of lines drawn on its surface. Perhaps he even thought of his curves first in the form of ratios, and then, having ascertained that these ratios apply to the cone, in the form of conic sections. His solution of the Delos problem, at the very least, starts from an equation and not, like Archytas' solution, from the stereometric interpretation of a mechanism.

Menaechmus proposed two related solutions. In the first the required means are found by the intersection of a hyperbola and a parabola. In the second they are found by the intersection of two parabolas. Both of them can be translated with ease into algebraic equations of the second degree.

Let us mark off the two given straight lines a and b on a co-ordinate system, and let us suppose that the problem is solved by extending a and b to form x and y respectively in such a way that $x > b$.

First solution

By the statement of the problem $\dfrac{a}{y} = \dfrac{y}{x} = \dfrac{x}{b}$

From one side of the equation, we have $xy = ab$ which is that of a hyperbola with o as its centre and x and y as asymptotes.

From the other side of the equation, $by = x^2$ which is that of a parabola with o for its vertex, y for axis and b for *latus rectum*.

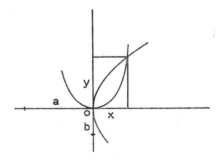

Thus, a and b being the given magnitudes, we must construct in succession a hyperbola having o as its centre, whose distances to the co-ordinates, multiplied by one another, give a product equal to ab, and then a parabola having o as its vertex, the ordinate for axis and b for *latus rectum*. The intersection of the two curves gives values of x and y satisfying both equations at once.

Second solution

It was given that
$$\frac{a}{y} = \frac{y}{x} = \frac{x}{b}$$
From one part, we have $by = x^2$, as before.
From the other part, the equation $ax = y^2$
which is that of a second parabola with o for vertex, x for axis and a for *latus rectum*

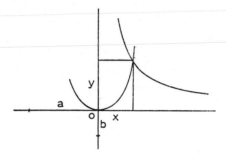

As in the first solution, the intersection of the two curves gives values of x and y satisfying both equations at once.

Such was Menaechmus' double solution. It appeared so unlike the modes of thought characteristic of the mathematicians of the Academy that certain modern historians have thought it apochryphal. However, its authenticity has not been questioned here, since it is guaranteed by Eratosthenes' explicit testimony. What makes it appear so different is the fact that it lends itself too easily to a modern interpretation using analytical geometry. But if we disregard the terms parabola and hyperbola, which were introduced only later, and replace the algebraic equations by the long formulae for calculating proportions, we shall find ourselves back among methods of thought familiar to Euclid's pre-decessors. The idea of the geometrical locus is itself a product of the typical bent of axiomatic mathematics, opening up from a simple definition (or, if one prefers it, from a different way of establishing a collection of relations) a whole host of new possibilities. Let us hasard the word: Menaechmus thought of a curve as the representation of a *function*, whilst ontological mathematics regarded it either as a figure or as the figure of a reality. In this respect, Menaechmus is in-disputably paving a way for modern mathematics: he is a modern. But all mathematics in Eudoxus' time pointed to the future, and in this prodigious change of perspective Menaechmus' views represent not so much an innovation as the most advanced stage that they had yet reached.

V

Astronomy : Eudoxus II

According to the unanimous judgment of antiquity, Eudoxus's astronomical discoveries were his main claim to glory. It appears that his interest in this science was awakened in Egypt. His observations on the star Canopus and on some constellations in the southern celestial hemisphere are a sure proof that he spent part of this time with the priests of Heliopolis in compiling a map of the sky. Three and a half centuries later travellers were still shown the building, south of the great city on the shores of the Nile, which he used as an observatory. As well as the layout of the heavens he made a study of the calendar. He not only recorded with care the times of rising and setting of the stars but also noted down the dates on which the Nile rose and fell, the dates of the religious festivals, and those when the first signs of the changing seasons—that is, the meteorological variations— became apparent. He filled out his own notes with information from the priests. From them, for instance, he obtained an explanation of the working of the Egyptian calendar, which differed greatly from the Greek calendar in comprising twelve equal months of thirty days and intercalating five additional days at the end of the year, without making any allowance for the quarter-day additional to the 365, as a result of which all the dates of the festivals, even the seasonal ones, fell back one day every fourth year. He even kept a daily record of the weather, so that we can read in the universal calendar that he published some twenty years later entries of the following sort:

> 12 March: setting of the Pleiades. The star of Hera is the colour of fire. Signs of a change in the weather. The south wind is blowing, and if it blows a gale it burns up the fruits of the soil.[1]

In addition, the Egyptian priests seem to have given him a brief account of the principles of Chaldean astrology, but his fundamental rationalism made these objectionable to him:

> When the Chaldeans draw from each individual's date of birth prognostics and predictions about his life, we must not believe a word of what they say. (F 343)

Perhaps the most valuable lesson he learned from his stay in Egypt was the observational basis of astronomy. Once settled at Cyzicus, he carried on with the study of the sky he had begun on the banks of the Nile. The solution of the problems of the calendar remained the final goal towards which his research was leading, but he worked towards it slowly, and the first stages of this enterprise diverted him for the time being into very different studies. From this period, indeed, dates the book which had the most lasting influence on his contemporaries and on posterity: the *Phaenomena*.

The stellar sphere

The title of *Phaenomena* represents a programme in itself. From Eudoxus' time on, it became the usual practice to reserve this word, which means 'appearances', for a strictly astronomical meaning. In this sense it refers sometimes to the visible movements of the stars, sometimes to the aspect and arrangement of the constellations in the firmament. But the word did not have this special meaning before Eudoxus; and when he chose it as his title, two other senses of the term, each linked to a well-established tradition of

---

1. Quoted in a Greco-Egyptian calendar written on papyrus in Saïs, a town on the Nile Delta, around 310 B.C. (*Pap. Hibeh* I, 27). See also below, p. 140.

thought, gave an added breadth to its meaning. One of these traditions was that of Platonism. For Plato, *seeming* or *appearing* is mentally contrasted with *being*: the world of *appearances* is but the misleading reflection of the world of *essences*, which alone the philosopher's thought hopes to grasp. The other, older and more widespread tradition also contrasted *appearance* with *being*, but in such a way as to oppose the world of *visible* things to that of *hidden* things. Anaxagoras and Democritus, the last natural philosophers of the fifth century, and following them such famous doctors as Philistion of Locri and Diocles of Carystus, all of whose names were familiar to Eudoxus, happily justified their ideas by appealing to the axiom: 'Phenomena are glimpses of the invisible.'

In line with these two traditions of thought about the relation between truth and appearances, Eudoxus had the choice of regarding celestial phenomena either as the reflection of an ideal order, or as the visible aspect of an invisible reality. He could exclaim with Plato:

> We should use the broidery in the heaven as illustrations to facilitate the study which aims at those higher objects, just as we might employ, if we fell in with them, diagrams drawn and elaborated with exceptional skill by Daedalus or any other artist or draughtsman: for I take it that any one acquainted with geometry who saw such diagrams would indeed think them most beautifully finished but would regard it as ridiculous to study them seriously in the hope of gathering from them true relations of equality, doubleness, or any other ratio. ... Hence we shall pursue astronomy, as we do geometry, by means of problems, and we shall dispense with the starry heavens, if we propose to obtain a real knowledge of astronomy, and by that means to convert the natural intelligence of the soul from a useless to a useful possession. (*Republ.* 529 DE and 530 B)

But he could alternatively adopt the outlook of the astronomers whose ideas Plato criticized in the same passage as materialistic:

In the matter of the proportion which the night bears to the day, both these to the month, the month to the year, and the other stars to the sun and moon and to one another, will he not regard as absurd the man who supposes these things, which are corporeal and visible, to be changeless and subject to no aberrations of any kind: and will he not hold it absurd to exhaust every possible effort to apprehend their true condition? (*Republ.* 530 A)

Plato's astronomy could not suit Eudoxus. Even granting that at this time he had not yet embarked on the geometrical problems which would soon lead him to turn his back on ontological mathematics, his medical training taught him that appearances, though they may be misleading, are the only available indications of empirical truth. The medical school of Cnidus, that great rival of Hippocrates' school, cultivated a basically empirical tradition, which we know to have been characterized from the start by a rigorous observation of symptoms, aimed at recognizing the differences between various illnesses. Although they had no great range of treatments, the doctors of Cnidus carried their descriptions of appearances to great lengths: they wished to diagnose with certainty. For a scholar trained in this discipline, as Eudoxus was, Plato's professed mistrust of astronomers who based their hypotheses on the annual record of phenomena must have appeared a mistake, since it led one to reject the only tangible indication of the hidden reality, the only positive means of penetrating into the invisible world. Eudoxus was thus predisposed to adopt the traditional attitude of Greek science towards phenomena, rather than the new scepticism preached by Plato.

The *Phaenomena* is nothing more than a description of the visible sky. In it Eudoxus does not touch on the problem, how the stars and their movement are related to the constitution of the universe. But the title of his work does assert the importance of an exact knowledge of the observable facts. When he re-edited this same description later on, for the benefit of his Cnidian compatriots, he gave it the even more telling name of *The Mirror*, presenting the starry sky as a reflection of the world. However, he did not refrain from resorting to a preconceived notion of the shape of the universe. He assumes without discussion that the earth represents the centre of the world, and that the stars are fixed to the interior of a hollow sphere which turns on an axis passing through the pole star and the earth. Part of the book is even given over to demonstrating, in the layout of the constellations, the existence of this sphere; this must be interpreted as a sort of verification of commonly accepted ideas. But that apart, nothing in the *Phaenomena* gives any hint of the subsequent development of his astronomical theories, or even suggests that a theory might arise from it. Indeed, it is as though Eudoxus himself did not know what vision of the universe would later be revealed to him.

The book comprises three chapters following an introduction of which practically nothing remains. The first describes the sky in the manner of a geographical map, locating the constellations in relation to one another, from the pole star as far as the extreme stars in the southern hemisphere visible in Egypt. The second chapter returns to the celestial map and locates the constellations once again, this time in relation to the principal circles of the sphere: the north polar circle, the tropics, the equator, the approaches to the circle of 'perpetual invisibility' (the southern circle), as well as two last circles passing through the poles, one at the longitude of Cyzicus and Cnidus, the other at right angles to the first. The third chapter, and much the longest, compiles a list of the stars which rise above or sink below the horizon at the beginning of each month. This last chapter, worked out with the greatest care, was to form the basis of an astronomical calendar which served as a standard for the numerous so-called 'luni-solar' calendars used in the various Greek towns. We know, for example, that it was used in this way by Philip of Opus, the disciple of Plato, and by several others.

Though this work had considerable success at the start, and though it stimulated several imitations during the fourth century and could still, early in the following century, inspire verse by verse the astronomical poem which Aratus of

Soli quite specifically entitled *Phaenomena,* and which was famous throughout antiquity, it is known to us today only by way of quotations, which are fortunately fairly numerous. One element is completely lost—the illustrations. Eudoxus speaks of the constellations as if his reader knew their shapes: he never describes them. Does this mean that his book was illustrated with drawings and maps, as were several manuals of astronomy from the sixth century B.C. on? Or did he assume that his reader possessed either a celestial sphere, or a map of the sky, such as were available from the end of the fifth century? There is no way of knowing. We may simply remark that the first chapter describes the firmament as if it were set out on a circular map in polar projection: the pole star and the two Bears in the centre, surrounded by the constellations of the northern hemisphere, then the circle of the equator three-fifths of the way along the radius of the map, and finally, between this circle and the edge of the map, the constellations of the southern hemisphere. Several maps of this form have been handed down to us through ancient manuscripts: it is possible that they are derived from a pattern bequeathed by Eudoxus to posterity, or from an even older example which he had in front of him.

While relying on the presence of a map, Eudoxus still describes the constellations just as he sees them in the sky. When he describes Cepheus, for instance, he explains that he has his head *at the bottom* and his feet *over* the tail of the Little Bear, having in mind the actual arrangement of these patterns for a terrestrial observer, and not their reproduction on a map. Similarly, when he describes Hercules, with his left knee on the ground and his right leg forward, he is regarding the constellation in its actual position in the firmament, with body turned facing the observer. If he had described it from a celestial sphere, such as that supporting the statue of 'Atlas Farnese' in the Naples Museum, he would have shown the back view of Hercules, in the same way that the engraver of the medal on p. 142 represented Perseus. Indeed, although sculptors claimed to reproduce on spheres of this kind the appearance of the firmament located outside the universe, custom required them to present the figures in front view, even at the risk of confusing left and right. These two examples are thus a proof that Eudoxus gave priority to direct observation, and that the use of a map or a sphere played no part in his descriptive work.

Being a purely descriptive work, the *Phaenomena* is interesting chiefly to the historian of ancient astronomy, though certain statements in it have also given modern astronomers the chance to compare the state of the sky in his day with its present state. From the more general standpoint of the history of ideas, once Eudoxus' purpose is known, an actual reading of the surviving texts does not offer any notable surprises. So we need quote here only the few fragments which touch upon fundamental questions.

The first of these is at the beginning of the book, immediately after the succinct description of the celestial sphere and of the fixed axis of the universe:

> There is a certain star which always remains in the same spot, and this star is the pole of the universe. (Fr. 11)

Some twenty years later, the navigator Pytheas of Marseilles was to assert, on the contrary, that there is no star at the pole, but an empty space surrounded by three stars roughly forming three angles of a square. The star known nowadays as the pole star was then about thirteen degrees away from the pole. How can such a mistake be accounted for? Eudoxus' way of specifying his pole star implies that he does not link it to any of the neighbouring constellations, Great Bear, Little Bear or Dragon. So it is not a simple matter of his failing to appreciate the exact position of the pole. Rather one must allow that he locates the pole in the correct place, and then imagines the existence of the star, having a preconceived idea that the pivot of the sky must be marked in that way. So he hesitates between a radical application of the empirical method, which would have led him to declare that there was no visible star at the pole, and a concession to the logic of things. We shall come across another example of this slightly ambiguous attitude in due course.

Another fragment of the first chapter is worth quoting,

since it allows us to compare his two successive editions, the *Phaenomena* and the *Mirror*.

> First version: A short distance below Perseus and Cassiopea is the head of the Great Bear. The stars in the region between these constellations are of weak luminosity. (Fr. 36)
>
> Second version: *Behind* Perseus and *alongside the hips of* Cassiopea, a short distance *away*, *is found* the head of the Great Bear. The *intermediate* stars are of weak luminosity. (Fr. 37)

In his first observation, Eudoxus had placed the Great Bear too low. The version in the *Mirror*, while improving the style, also corrects the error, and specifies the position more precisely. The reference to stars 'of weak luminosity', common to both versions, is an innovation in Greek astronomy. It inaugurates a classification of stars according to their brightness which has left its mark, by way of antiquity and the Arab astronomers, on modern astronomy. Eudoxus, it is true, did not yet think of classifying the stars according to their magnitudes: he merely attributed them to their constellations. In another passage, he characterized the star located between the front paws of the Great Bear as 'brilliant', and the one visible below the back paws as 'more brilliant'.

When describing the constellations in his first chapter, Eudoxus projects them (as it were) on a planisphere, without however invoking the as yet unknown rules of stereographic projection. The second chapter, on the other hand, re-establishes them in their real positions, and locates them precisely on the circles of the celestial sphere. Eudoxus had two purposes in mind here. On the one hand he wanted to create a system of celestial co-ordinates which would make possible the scientific production of the sky-maps employed, for example, by navigators. On the other hand, having an eye to observations bearing on the movements of the sun, the earth and the planets, he wanted to be able to refer to these circles as datum-lines easily and at any time of the year, by way of the stars which mark them out. He is generally content to list the parts of the constellations crossed or touched by them. In two passages, however, he goes further, and offers the reader a more significant thought. These are the following:

> The sun also [that is, as well as the moon] is observed to make a variation in the neighbourhood of the tropics, though this is much less apparent to the eye and is extremely small. (Fr. 63)

> The tropic of the summer solstice is divided in such a way that the arc passing above the earth is to the arc passing below the earth in the ratio of 12 to 7 [or of 5 to 3, according to the version in the *Mirror*]. (Fr. 67)

The first of these two quotations comes from the *Mirror*. What bearing does it have on the circles, and why is it missing from the *Phaenomena*? By way of introduction to his second chapter, Eudoxus explained briefly his division of the celestial sphere by circles. In the *Phaenomena*, he merely drew the attention of his readers to the fact that these circles were no more than lines of construction, imaginary and devoid of width, simple boundaries to the zones of the sky: the arctic circle defines the zone in which the stars never fall' below the horizon, the summer tropic is the latitude at which the sun sets at the moment of the summer solstice, and so on. But between the publication of the *Phaenomena* and that of the *Mirror* one can date an observation from which Eudoxus saw that the latitude in which the sun sets at the solstice, and that in which the moon sets on the anniversary dates of the lunar calendar vary slightly, sometimes towards the north, sometimes towards the south. This most important observation was later to result in additional spheres being introduced into the explanation of the movements of the stars, but it is introduced into the *Mirror* merely to warn the reader that the tropic can be determined only within a certain approximation. Actually he was mistaken, but this care to take a new observation or consideration into account is typical of his entirely positive attitude towards the data of experience.

The second quotation comes from the *Phaenomena*, and its variant from the *Mirror*. It indicates for us the quality of

Eudoxus' measurements in the clearest—and at the same time the most alarming—manner. For consider: the ratio of the periods assumed in the version written at Cyzicus corresponds to a terrestrial latitude of 42°14′10″. This latitude actually passes about 130 miles further north. As for the latitude assumed for Cnidus in the *Mirror*, 40°51′27″, this corresponds roughly to that of Istanbul, with an error of nearly 310 miles. Expressed in degrees, the difference between the two latitudes is 1°22′43″. Taking the circumference of 400,000 stades—say, 41,800 miles—which Eudoxus attributed to the terrestrial sphere (as another work tells us), this arc is equal to a distance of 175 miles, instead of the 250 miles which would be the true distance between Cyzicus and Cnidus given the same circumference. Evidently, then, astronomical measurements could not in such a case be checked against terrestrial or maritime distance measurements. Finally, when one discovers that Eudoxus placed Athens on the same latitude as Cnidus, and that this estimate was not disputed by the geographers of the succeeding generation, although the error was nearly fifteen minutes of arc, one realizes that this series of errors must be due, not to the negligence or the observer, but to the inadequacy of his measuring instruments.

And, indeed, how could he measure and compare the lengths of the night and the day? The method he describes in his treatise *On the extinction of the stars by the sun* (see below, p. 136), failing any other information, suggests an operation such as the following. Having filled the upper section of a clepsydra with water, he took the stopper out at sunrise and left it until sunset to empty itself into the lower section, topping up the water as often as was necessary. Taking the receptacles into which all the water had flowed during the day, he poured it once again through the clepsydra between sunset and sunrise. The comparison of the quantities which had run away during the day and the night, as measured by weight or by volume, gave the relative lengths of day and night. Using such a procedure, as with any procedure involving a clepsydra, evaporation alone—to say nothing of the irregular rate of the flow, and the problems of pouring water between containers—was enough to introduce a difference between the rate of consumption of water by night and by day, so apparently lengthening the day at the expense of the night. Eudoxus, however, appears later on to have given up attempting to establish latitudes by comparing the duration of day and night. His *Circuit of the Earth* seems to make use of the idea of *climate*—probably his own discovery—this term alluding to the *angle* between the sun's rays and the vertical. However, even if he had recognized this earlier, it is not certain that he would have made use of it to improve his time-measurements at the solstices: the full implications of the inter-relations between geography and astronomy, particularly the astronomical calendar, did not at once impress themselves on the Greek mathematicians.

The third chapter is the most important of the book, in that it lays the foundations of an astral calendar. The astral year is divided into twelve months whose beginnings are marked by the appearance on the horizon at a given time, in succession, of the twelve constellations of the zodiac. We know that, by the *rising* of a sign, Eudoxus referred not to the appearance of its first star, but to the passage of the middle of the sign across to the line of the horizon. In this way he was less likely to make mistakes, since the identification of the still invisible constellation from its first star to rise would have been fraught with uncertainty. For all his lack of satisfactory instruments, he at least had a feel for astronomical observation. This part of his work, like the preceding one, consists of wearisome lists: all the poetic ingenuity of Aratus was required to transform it successfully into tolerable verse. I will quote just one example, the shortest:

When the Fishes [Pisces] rise, one can see rising along with them, among the northern constellations, the rest of Andromeda, the right-hand side of Perseus, the Triangle which is above the Ram; and among the southern constellations the head of the southern Fish. One can see setting at the same time among the southern constellations the Altar and the rest of Hydra; among the northern constellations, none is setting. (Fr. 110–111)

The version in the *Mirror*, preserved in this chapter for this passage alone, introduces a modification in the case of Perseus: 'More or less the whole of Perseus.' This variation is evidence that Eudoxus had meticulously repeated all his observations at Cnidus, and that he had noted the consequent differences with the greatest care. A somewhat less explicit testimony seems also to indicate that he included in the *Mirror* the dates when Canopus, which is visible only at Cnidus, appeared on the horizon. The text of the *Phaenomena* still refers to this star as 'the star visible in Egypt'.

The astral calendar

How was the *Phaenomena*, and particularly the last chapter, to help in the establishment of a calendar? The problem which preoccupied the aediles of all the Greek cities was to provide their constituents with a public calendar which, while allowing of an integral number of days and months in the year and giving each month a length approximating to one cycle of the moon, should not depart bit by bit from the astral year, with the irritating consequence of progressively displacing the fixed feast-days away from the seasonal events they were supposed to celebrate. The only acceptable solution was for the calendar to be adjusted periodically against the astral year by the regular or occasional intercalation of additional days. In theory, it would have been sufficient to make the civic months equal in length to the zodiacal months. But the zodiacal months involve fractions of a day, incompatible with the practical purposes of the civic calendar. What is more, the custom of counting the civic months by the cycles of the moon was too deeply rooted in popular custom for it to be completely abandoned. The astronomers in all the cities were thus reduced to checking and correcting the local calendars whenever they seemed to be deviating too far from reality. A calendar fixing the dates of the rising and setting of the constellations and of the most easily identifiable stars was therefore indispensable to them.

The *Phaenomena* did not provide this calendar, even for the latitude of Cyzicus for which it had been composed. Indeed, the observation of risings and settings coinciding

with the appearance of a particular sign of the zodiac above
the horizon can be made at any moment of the night and
on any day of the year, at least within limits. It is not restricted to coincidences between the rising of the sign and
the rising or setting of the sun. However, it is practicable
only well into the night, when the horizon is not lit up owing
to the proximity of the sun. But if one wanted to verify a
date in the civic calendar by the rising or setting of a star, it
was necessary to choose the star which rose or set exactly
at the moment when the civic day began—that is to say, at
sunset, for the Greeks at that time followed the custom
which still prevails in Jewish communities today. The
observation of the star had thus to take place during the
first hour of darkness, just as soon as the star was visible, and
the observer had to satisfy himself that the distance which
the star had travelled between its emergence above the
horizon and the point reached at its first moment of visi-
bility corresponded to the time which had elapsed since
the disappearance of the sun. This observational problem
called for the closest attention.

It must first be noted that the appearance of a star on the
horizon is difficult to mark with precision, even in the absence
of all luminosity. By the time it is perceived, it has always
risen a few degrees already. Its setting is easier to fix, though
if the horizon is still lightened by the glimmer of dusk, the
observation is impracticable, and by the time it is possible
the star has already disappeared. In order to get round these
difficulties and establish rules guaranteeing a high degree
of precision at all seasons and in all circumstances, Eudoxus
composed a special treatise entitled *On the extinction of the
stars by the sun*. We possess a distant recollection of this, from
a manual of practical astronomy of somewhat later date, in
the form of the following instruction:

> At the moment when the sun sets, the stars are not
> immediately visible. They can be seen only when the
> sun has dropped below the horizon by a distance equal
> to half a sign of the zodiac, that is to say after half-an-
> hour. Experimental demonstration: at the moment of
> sunset, let water run from a clepsydra into a receptacle

up till the moment when the stars appear. Then, as the stars begin to rise, pour the water back into the clepsydra and let it run out once again right to the last drop. The complete sign will leave the horizon at the precise moment when the container empties. (Fr. 128)

By applying this practical rule and looking up the correspondence between the observed star and the rising of a sign of the zodiac in the third chapter of the *Phaenomena* or the *Mirror*, any astronomer was in a position to check the dates of the calendar entrusted to his care, and even to compose for himself an astral calendar establishing the coincidences between the local feast-days and the rising and setting of a particular star. All he need do was, first, to set out in a synoptic table the risings of the signs of the zodiac, so as conveniently to determine the months of the astral year; then, to record for each of these risings the names of the stars which rose or set on the same day; and finally, to note down in the course of the year the day in any zodiacal month on which a particular easily recognizable star rose or set. In practice, this list would not contain the names of all the constellations described by Eudoxus, but only those which had been long familiar to farmers and sailors: Sirius, Arcturus, Orion, etc. Once this astral calendar had been drawn up, the astronomer would add solar dates to it also: the beginning of the civic year, equinoxes and solstices, beginnings of the seasons, etc. After one year of conscientious observation, the local astronomical calendar was established. We know that Philip of Opus composed such a one on the basis of the *Phaenomena*, and tradition preserves an accurate recollection of other similarly-based labours in Philip's entourage.

When some sort of order had been introduced into the astronomical calendar, in the way here described, for the latitude of the locality in question, a second task began: the adjustment of the civic calendar to conform with this calendar. Like most peoples in antiquity, the Greeks marked the months of the year not by the passage of the signs of the zodiac across the horizon, but by the periodic reappearance of the new moon. This system had the irreplaceable advantage of allowing those without a calendar at their disposal to keep count of the months, but also the serious drawback of making the year too short by about ten days. As most of the religious feasts were fixed by relation to this lunar register, it was practically impossible to give it up. The municipal authorities were generally content to reduce its ill-effects by adding one whole cycle of the moon to certain years. The counting of the days in the month—twenty-nine or thirty—and the selection of the years destined to contain an extra month varied considerably from one city to another, and it was also necessary in every city to correct from time to time the deviations in the civic calendar not eliminated by the intercalated months. From the sixth century, however, an eight-yearly rhythm of insertions can be observed more or less everywhere. The intercalated month was added to three years in an eight-year cycle: for example, in the third, the sixth and the eighth. The eight years thus amounted to ninety-nine months having sometimes twenty-nine, sometimes thirty days, and the total of 2921, 2922 or 2923 days—depending on the solutions adopted—covered pretty well the length of eight theoretical solar years of $365\frac{1}{4}$ days. Yet in practice these eight-year cycles were rarely adhered to strictly, and it was frequently necessary to get them corrected with the help of the astronomers. The *Phaenomena*, the *Mirror*, and the astronomical calendars based on these works by Philip of Opus and others, were the means by which this was achieved.

A little later we find Eudoxus himself extracting from the *Phaenomena* and the *Mirror* an astronomical calendar of a new type. The composition of this important work probably took place after his return to Cnidus, and formed part of the general programme of legislative and administrative reforms which Eudoxus was instructed to carry out after the overthrow of the oligarchy, the re-establishment of the democracy, and the removal of the city of Cnidus from the creek where it had been located since ancient times to the open sea. But the scope of this calendar, which seems to have been given the title of the *Octaeteris* (plagiarized later by several other similar calendars), goes far beyond the requirements of municipal administration. In an introduction which recalls briefly the principles governing the establishment of an astronomical calendar for any given latitude, Eudoxus specified for the benefit of his readers observations which would be necessary in order to make his calendar usable in other latitudes: the procedure for determining the solstices by the length of the shadow of the *gnomon*[1], for calculating the respective lengths of the day and night throughout year, for registering local feast-days, etc. He also noted the years in the eight-year cycle when an extra month could conveniently be inserted, though without entering into detail about the different systems of lunar months characteristic of the civic calendars then current. His eight-year cycle seems to have contained 2921 days; the method of intercalation adopted is not known. Moreover, taking advantage of his Egyptian records, he added to his Greek data all the information of particular relevance to Egypt, for example the dates of the rise and fall of the Nile, and those of certain religious feasts. He seems to have added to this such meteorological notes as he was able to collect from the old Athenian calendars, taking care to mention their origin, with the result that his work acquired a universal character.

This calendar was not preserved for very long in its original form. Taken by this happy idea, an anonymous author published a much more voluminous *Octaeteris*, less than twenty years after the death of the astronomer of Cnidus, which added to Eudoxus' data others from more ancient and more recent calendars, along with observations allegedly collected from the Magi of Chaldea and from the Indian Sadhu Calanis, newly fashionable as a consequence of Alexander's expedition. All we know of Eudoxus' *Octaeteris* has come down to us by way of this compilation—whose author, moreover, sheltered under the name of the famous man who inspired him. Probably the phrase 'the Art of Eudoxus', which sometimes refers to the science of the calendar, appeared for the first time in this apochryphal work.

1. The gnomon was originally the needle—or style—of the horizontal sundial. Imported into Greece from Babylon in the sixth century by Anaximander of Miletus, it was used up to Eudoxus' time only in solar clocks.

It is no exaggeration to say that we owe our modern calendar to Eudoxus, through the intermediary of the second *Octaeteris*. This compilation had, indeed, an immense success. By about the year 310, barely ten years after its publication, we can already detect its influence at Saïs, one of the capitals of the Nile Delta, which was then becoming hellenized. A local calendar, written in Greek, reconstructs in its preface a shortened version of the introduction, and describes the additional observations carried out according to these instructions so as to allow for the special conditions in Egypt. The little book contains many slips, providing representative evidence of the cheap cultural level of the groups for which the *Octaeteris* had been particularly conceived. The author did not dare to sign his modest work, and the respect with which he refers to the book which had inspired him—albeit in fallacious terms—shows how conscious he is of his debt to Greek science.

At that time there came to Saïs a man of the highest wisdom, who needed my services, for I have lived in this district for five years. He explained everything to me, and showed me how to work with the stone tablet which is called in Greek a *gnomon*. He taught me that there are two circuits of the sun, one which determines the night and the day, and the other which separates winter from summer [etc.]. (Papyrus of Hibeh I 27 l.19 ff.)

A century or so later, the author of an astronomical handbook entitled *Teaching about the Sky*, with the sub-title *The Art of Eudoxus*, pilfers once again from the *Octaeteris*, and on a much larger scale. Among a jumble of banalities taken from this work, a few pieces of information catch one's attention as being directly relevant to Eudoxus. Here, indeed, we learn how he divided up the year: 91 days from the summer solstice to the autumn equinox, 92 from then to the winter solstice, 91 to the spring equinox and 91 till the summer solstice, or 92 in the intercalary years. This addition, naturally, involves only the movement of the sun against the stars, and has nothing to do with lunar months.

The Saïs calendar and this manual must be regarded as the tangible outcome of the second *Octaeteris*, which was designedly a work of popularization. But on the scientific plane, also, this work had its influence. Around the year 230 Eratosthenes was already producing an important commentary on it. Near the same time, the astronomer Dositheus of Pelusium, a pupil of the famous Conon of Alexandria, published under the same title a new universal calendar, which collected all the traditional data once again, and added some fresh information on the same subjects. This is the third identifiable *Octaeteris*, and there were probably others. Simultaneously, the influence of the second was spreading among the most ancient centres of Greek culture, notably at Miletus, where archæologists brought to light the relics of a public calendar which is an extract from it and has preserved its literary style. This calendar is of the type called a *parapegma*: beside each datum—the rising of a star, an item of meteorological information, a quotation of Eudoxus or another author, etc.—a hole was drilled into the rock, intended to hold a peg which it was the business of a municipal official to move each day, so as to mark the date. Illustrating yet again how Eudoxus' ingenuity was applied to practical ends, the chance discovery of this *parapegma* entitles us to imagine that similar ones would have been found in the public square of numerous cities. Thanks to the widening influence of the *Octaeteris*, the principles of the astral calendar thus tended gradually to displace the traditional 'luni-solar' calendars. During the first century B.C. Rome in its turn enters into its sphere of influence, and the institution of the Julian calendar by Caesar, in 46 B.C., definitely establishes the acceptance by the West of the ideas which Eudoxus had first put into circulation three centuries earlier. Transformed after several improvements into the Gregorian calendar in A.D. 1582, the calendar of Julius Caesar served as it were as a bridge between the Hellenistic reorganization of the *Octaeteris* and the system in use at the present day. Thus we find ourselves directly benefiting from the astronomer of Cnidus' initiative in making possible the general employment of the astral year:

he has no more solid claim to universal admiration than this.

In the same realm of practical considerations, Eudoxus is the author of another remarkable invention: the plane astrolabe. Unfortunately we have very little information about this other application of his astronomical work. The instrument in question was known to antiquity by the name of the 'spider's web', a name later confined to one part only of the newer types of astrolabe. Vitruvius, who had only read of it and had no other knowledge of it, classified it among clocks. It was used, then, to tell the time, but probably only by night. A fragment of a much later plane astrolabe in bronze discovered at Salzburg gives an approximate idea of its mode of operation (see the figure below). The principal constellations of the northern hemisphere

were marked on a disc, whose centre was meant to correspond to the pole star, the constellations of the zodiac being
marked along the edge. This edge, defined by a circular
line, was in addition perforated with a ring of holes corresponding to the days of the year; the Salzburg disc contains
182 or 183 holes in all: namely one hole for two days, and
fifteen for a sign of the zodiac. A peg was pushed in to
mark the actual place of any particular day in the zodiacal
month.

How could this instrument indicate the time? Let us
suppose that the disc was mounted on a pivot at the bottom
of a cylindrical box and that its lid had been replaced by
the *spider's web*, that is to say by a network of threads joining
the centre to the circumference. With the disc representing
the starry sky and the web indicating the hours, all that was
required was to make the former follow the motion of the
stars, and its position relative to the fixed threads of the web
would designate the required hour throughout the night.
In the Salzburg astrolabe, this movement was probably
effected by some sort of motor, so that the disc completed
a whole turn in twenty-four hours. This is why the marking
of the constellations on its surface only plays a decorative
role. But in Eudoxus' day the owner of the instrument had,
for the lack of a motor, to turn the disc himself on each con-
sultation to the position corresponding to the state of the
sky at the moment of observation. His procedure was thus
like that of a tourist who orientates a geographical map: he
turned the disc until the constellations engraved on its
surface took up positions matching those of the corresponding
constellations visible in the sky at that precise moment. But
since the stars rise at different times, varying with the day of
the year, it was also necessary to relate the position of the
disc exactly to the particular day. This was the function
of the peg: fixed each evening in the hole corresponding to
that day, it represented the position of the sun in the sign
of the zodiac observable on the horizon at the same moment,
and during the night, in proportion as the disc was rotated
to follow the movement of the stars, it acted as an 'hour-
hand'. Let us suppose again that the astrolabe had to be

used in different latitude from Cnidus, it could then be regulated according to the instructions of the local astral calendar, which would indicate the entry of the sun into the signs of the zodiac or, failing that, at least the dates on which the principal stars rose exactly at sunset.

The theory of the spheres

Having noted the decisive advance which Eudoxus' observations gave to the science of the calendar (which is the proper subject of *astronomy*, in the ancient sense of the word), let us go back and consider their effect on that other science (called *astrology* in antiquity) which studies the structure of the universe, particularly the movements of the sun, the moon and the planets.

What was known about this subject at the time when the *Phaenomena* appeared? During earlier centuries several theories had held the attention of the educated public in turn, and had gradually implanted in the popular imagination some rudimentary ideas about the organization of the cosmos. Despite considerable variations, their general effect was to popularize the image of a spherical or hemispherical universe, with the earth at its centre and the starry vault as its boundary. In the sixth century, the movement of the Sun and Moon, and sometimes those of the planets also, had been explained in a number of ways. By the time of Plato, they had become the physicists' central preoccupation. Plato himself repeatedly displayed his interest in this part of astronomy, though he never gave it a preponderant importance and never developed any really original ideas about it. He deals with the subject chiefly in the *Timaeus*, which describes the creation of the world, setting out concisely the mutual relations of physics, philosophical speculation and theology in a system which, while novel in certain respects, in general follows faithfully the accepted views of his time. The resulting synthesis can perhaps be regarded as representative of the state of the science before the researches of Eudoxus, and is interesting enough to deserve a brief explanation.

In shape Plato's universe is a hollow sphere. This sphere

is carried round the axis of the world in a uniform rotational movement by a circle fixed to its internal face and constituting its equator. A second circle, that of the zodiac, is fastened to the inside of the first by a common diameter, but moves in a different plane, corresponding to the ecliptic. The intersection of the two circles determines four angles, opposed in pairs and marking out a recumbent figure on the internal face of the sphere. (See the passage quoted on p. 163 below.) These two circles constitute the soul of the world, and are the ultimate source of the movements of the universe. The first carries the second around with it, but the second has in addition its own proper rotation, in the opposite direction, round an imaginary axis passing through its centre. In this way, any point chosen at random on its circumference is found, by the combination of the two movements, to describe a slow spiral in a direction opposite to that of the first circle. Further inside, the region between the second circle and the immobile Earth at the centre of the world is shared by six concentric circles of different sizes. The ratios of their respective radii to that of the zodiacal circle are, in succession, as 1, 2, 3, 4, 8 and 9 to 27. Each of these circles carries a heavenly body on its circumference. Nearest to the Earth is the circle of the Moon; then come the Sun, Venus, Mercury, Mars and Jupiter; finally, Saturn is attached to the zodiacal circle.

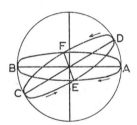

The above diagram helps to indicate how the movements of Plato's circles combine. The outside sphere, carrying the stars and moved by the first circle (the circle of the equator, AEBF), bears them round from east to west and brings them back to their starting-point in the space of a day. The circle of the zodiac (CEDF), rotating in the opposite direction and communicating its movement to the six concentric circles (not shown in the diagram), determines the seasonal variations in latitude of the seven so-called *wandering* stars. But each of the six circles enjoys in addition an individual movement which accounts for the apparent irregularity of the planetary orbits. The Moon, the Sun, Mars, Jupiter and Saturn turn in the same direction as the circle of the zodiac (namely, from west to east), but much more slowly than they turn from east to west through the impulse they receive from the circle of the equator. Seen from the earth, they thus describe an orbit similar to that of the stars, but with a certain delay brought about by their contrary movement, and a certain obliquity due to the tilting of the ecliptic. Venus and Mars, by contrast, turn in a direction opposite to the movement of the zodiac: namely, from east to west. In allotting them a track contrary to that which the zodiacal circle causes the Sun to follow (disregarding the movement received from the equatorial circle), Plato hoped to explain how it comes about that these two planets sometimes precede and sometimes follow the Sun, without ever moving far away from it. But, however one interprets the confused text of the *Timaeus*, this tentative explanation does not account for the actual facts.

Following Plato's example and guided by the *Timaeus*, several astronomers were soon looking for ways of correcting the most obvious inadequacies of his system. Philip of Opus puts forward an improved version in the *Epinomis*. The *Laws*, prepared by Plato shortly before his death, already alludes to attempts of the same general kind. Without doubt the *Timaeus* provoked an extraordinary craze for celestial mechanics and concentric circles. There is further evidence of this in a dialogue composed about the same time by Plato's pupil, Heraclides of Pontus: this presented a debate between a number of astronomers meeting at the Academy, with Plato himself intervening in the dialogue to prescribe for the assembled scientists the limits of their speculation.

To respect the observed facts[1] relating to the movements of the wandering stars, while assuming that
these movements are circular, unvarying and of con-
stant speed. (Quoted from Heraclides by Eudemus, in
his *History of Astronomy*.)

According to Heraclides, certain astronomers had already
attempted by this time to interpret this rule in the broadest
sense, some of them going so far (for instance) as to put
forward a theory of eccentric circles, and others suggesting
that the Earth rotates on an axis passing through its poles.
Evidently they had been prepared to resort without hesi-
tation to solutions of the greatest audacity.

The theory which Eudoxus developed must be seen within the framework of this extraordinary outburst of astronomical research. There are reasons for thinking that Heraclides did not overlook it in his dialogue, and even that he
may have expounded it there immediately after Plato's
introductory statement. Whether this was actually so or not,
it is clear that the theory scrupulously conformed to the
double recommendation which Heraclides put into the
philosopher's mouth: Eudoxus, as we shall see, makes
exclusive use of concentric spheres in uniform, continuous
movement, and more than any other of his colleagues he
bowed before the facts of observation.

We have seen above with what care he set himself,
throughout his stay at Cyzicus, to noting the daily positions
of the constellations, and what importance he attached to
determining exactly the state of the sky at sunrise and sunset. While these patient labours were to find their first
justification in the improvement of the calendar, it can be
demonstrated that Eudoxus drew on them equally for his
astronomical theory. Indeed, only a complete knowledge of
the layout of the stars for every day of the year can explain
how he was able to calculate the periods of the planetary
revolutions with scarcely any error, both the so-called

1. The first words of this rule were often translated by the expression 'saving
the appearances', which has an altogether different meaning. The precise
sense of the Greek is 'preserving the phenomena', thereby clearly indicating
the observed movements of the stars.

zodiacal periods, i.e. those which bring the planets back to the same position relative to the stars, and the so-called *synodic* periods, i.e. those which bring them back to the same position relative to the sun. The table below, which gives Eudoxus' figures alongside those of modern astronomy, shows no significant deviations, except for the relative positions of Mars and the Sun, which are especially difficult to determine.

| | Zodiacal periods | | Synodic periods | |
	Eudoxus	Modern astronomy	Eudoxus	Modern astronomy
Saturn	30 years	29 years + 166 days	390 days	378 days
Jupiter	12 years	11 years + 315 days	390 days	399 days
Mars	2 years	1 year + 322 days	260 days	780 days
Mercury	1 year	1 year	110 days	116 days
Venus	1 year	1 year	570 days	584 days

The title Eudoxus gave to the work which he devoted to his theory is evidence of his desire to base it securely on these figures. For he entitled it *On Speeds*, by which he implied that the periods of revolution of the heavenly bodies have dictated the combinations of the movements he will describe —whereas Plato (for instance) arrived at these movements by an argument whose starting-point was the hypothetical concentric circles. This is not to say that the mechanical hypothesis did not play a large part in the working-out of Eudoxus' system: in fact, it was very important for it and gave rise once again to the same fundamental errors as afflicted Plato's system. For Eudoxus, however, this hypothesis was subordinate to the observations, whereas, when it first saw the light in Plato's work, it had had only a tenuous connection with the observations. Thus the substitution of spheres for the traditional circles was motivated by the discovery of lateral deviations in certain orbits, of a kind that cannot be explained in terms of rotations in the planes of the ecliptic and the celestial equator alone. The only preconceived ideas which prevailed in all attempts to explain the phenomena in terms of the observed facts alone were the central position of the Earth, its immobility and the celestial rotations. On these points, current opinion and the influence of the Academy imposed invincibly a view whose falsity could not be suspected.

We know the theory of the concentric spheres from a shortened version of the description given by Eudemus in his *History of Astronomy*. This shortened version throws no light on the mathematical aspects of the mechanism which Eudoxus had conceived, nor on his account of the reasons which had led him to reject the systems based on circles. But, on the arrangement and functioning of the spheres, it is perfectly clear and requires no commentary.

Eudoxus and other writers before him recognized that the Sun had three movements. First, it is carried along by the sphere of the fixed [lit. *not wandering*] stars from rising to setting. Secondly, it moves of its own accord in a contrary direction across the twelve signs of the zodiac. Thirdly, it deviates laterally from the circle which passes through the middle of these signs. This last movement was inferred from the fact that the Sun does not always set in the same place at the summer and winter solstices. So men concluded that it must be carried by three spheres.

These three spheres having a common centre, and this centre being also the centre of the universe, Eudoxus supposed that the first contains the two others and turns around an axis through the poles of the universe in the same direction and with the same period as the sphere of the fixed stars. The second sphere, smaller than the first but bigger than the last, turns from West to East around an axis perpendicular to the plane of the ecliptic. The smallest rotates in the same direction as the second but its axis is different; it must be represented as perpendicular to the plane of a great circle oblique to the plane of the great circle of the preceding sphere. It is this oblique great circle which is apparently described by the centre of the Sun as it is carried round by the smallest of the three spheres, to which it is fixed.

The delay introduced by this sphere is much less than that introduced by the sphere immediately surrounding it, which keeps its middle place between the first and the third on account of its size and location. The largest, however, at the same time as following the rotation of the sphere of the fixed stars, causes the other two to rotate with it, for the poles of the second are located upon it, while the poles of the third (which carries the Sun) are themselves located upon the second. The second in its turn, having the poles of the third located upon it, carries the latter along with its own rotation, and consequently carries along the Sun also. That is why it appears to move from East to West. If these two spheres (the middle-sized and smallest ones) were immobile in themselves, the Sun's rotation would have the same period as that of the universe. But, as they rotate in a direction opposite to the first, the falling-back of the Sun between one setting and the next adds a certain delay to this period.

Such are the movements of the Sun. As regards the Moon, Eudoxus arranged things partly in the same way, partly in a different way. He likewise allowed three spheres to move it, because it has three apparent motions. The first moves like the sphere of the fixed stars. The second rotates in a contrary direction around an axis perpendicular to the plane of the ecliptic, as for the Sun. The third no longer follows the same system as for the Sun; it has the same position as the third sphere of that system, but not the same movement, being carried along by a slow motion in the opposite direction to the second and the same direction as the first, around an axis perpendicular to the plane of the circle which the centre of the Moon appears to describe. This circle is inclined on the ecliptic at an angle corresponding to the Moon's largest deviation in latitude. Clearly the distance between the poles of the third sphere and those of the second, measured on the circumference of the great circle which one can think of as marked out by these poles is equal to one-half of the Moon's deviation in latitude. In Eudoxus' hypothesis the first sphere is responsible for the Moon's revolution from East to West, the second for its apparent delay on the ecliptic relative to the signs of the zodiac, and the third for the fact that it does not always reach its extreme positions to the North and South at the same points of the zodiac, but that these points are displaced continually in a direction contrary to the progression of the signs. The third sphere thus rotates in the same direction as the sphere of the fixed stars, and since the retrogradation during each zodiacal month is very small the movement of this sphere towards the West is supposed to be slow.

Such are the movements of the Moon. Now, as concerns the five planets; these are each moved by four spheres, of which the first and the second have the same position as the two first spheres of the sun and the moon. For each planet, indeed, there is a first sphere which encloses the three others and rotates from East to West around the axis of the universe with the same period as the sphere of the fixed stars, and a second sphere which has its poles on the first and rotates around this axis and the poles of the ecliptic from West to East in the time which the planet apparently takes to travel through the entire circle of the zodiac. Thus, for Mercury and Venus the revolution of the second sphere is completed in one year, for Mars in two years, for Jupiter in twelve and for Saturn in thirty years.

The two other spheres have the following movements. The third in each planetary system has its poles on the circle of the ecliptic described (in theory) on the second sphere. It rotates from South to North in the period of time separating one rising of the planet from the next, during which it passes through all its positions relative to the Sun. This is the period of the revolution which mathematicians call the *synodic* revolution. Since this differs from planet to planet, the third spheres are not isochronous among themselves: Venus accomplishes her revolution in nineteen months, Mercury in a hundred and ten days, Mars in eight months and twenty days, Jupiter and Saturn in nearly thirteen months. Such are the movements of each third sphere. As for the fourth spheres, those which carry the heavenly body, these have different poles for each planet and rotate in the plane of an oblique circle. Their revolution is completed in the same time as that of the third spheres, but they move in the opposite direction, from East to West. The oblique circle is inclined at an angle to the great circle of the third sphere, but with a different obliquity in each system.

Clearly, then, the first sphere, rotating with the sphere of the fixed stars, causes all the others whose poles are fixed one upon another to rotate with it, and as a result the star itself also. That is why each planet rises and sets. The second sphere causes it to pass through all the signs of the zodiac, since it turns around the poles of the ecliptic carrying the two remaining spheres and the planet also from one sign to the next in the time it takes such planet to complete its apparent zodiacal revolution. The third sphere, having its poles on the ecliptic of the second and rotating from South to North and from North to South, carries along with it the fourth sphere and also the heavenly body which is fixed upon the latter. This is responsible for its deviation in latitude. But not the third sphere only: for, so far as it was on the third sphere by itself, the planet would actually have arrived at the poles of the zodiac circle and would have come near to the poles of the universe; but, as things are, the fourth sphere, which turns about the poles of the inclined circle carrying the planet and rotates in the opposite sense to the third, i.e. from East to West, but in the same period, will prevent any considerable divergence on the part of the planet from the zodiac circle, and will cause the planet to describe about this same zodiac circle the curve called by Eudoxus the *hippopede*, so that the breadth of this curve will be the maximum amount of the planet in latitude, a view for which Eudoxus has been attacked.

This system of spheres adds up to twenty-six spheres for the seven heavenly bodies; namely, six for the Sun and Moon together, and twenty for the five planets. (Fr. 124)

By comparison with the astronomical system of the *Timaeus*, Eudoxus' system has two obvious advantages. In the first place, it offers a mechanism which is easy to understand, which is always the same, and which allows for every combination of directions of rotation, of speeds and of angles of inclination. In the period following the publication of the theory of the spheres, this advantage was so keenly felt that Eudoxus' two most famous successors, his pupil Callippus and the philosopher Aristotle, simply looked for ways of introducing the improvements they thought necessary by adding fresh spheres. In the second place, the system of the spheres can be matched very simply against the astronomical observations. Callippus in particular took advantage of this merit, adding two spheres to the solar complex so as to explain the unequal distribution of the equinoxes and solstices in the solar year (his observations gave the astonishingly accurate result of 94, 92, 89 and 90 days, beginning from the Spring equinox), two spheres to the lunar complex to explain the similar inequality of the movement of this body in longitude, and one sphere each to the systems of Mars, Venus and Mercury, probably in order to give a better account of the delicate phenomena of the retrogradations. His system thus included thirty-three spheres.

These two advantages represent cause and effect. If the system of rotations in two planes (equatorial and ecliptic) made popular by Plato had to be replaced by a spherical system involving a complete sheaf of different planes, this was because serious and scientific observation of the planetary rotations had finally revealed movements more numerous and more varied than had hitherto been imagined. The recognition of these movements is thus the cause which brought in its train the invention of a richer and more adaptable mechanism. With Eudoxus, we may say, experience becomes the point of departure for theory, and mathematical development is something which enters in only as one goes along. For, despite the apparent importance of purely hypothetical and speculative elements (namely, the uniformity of the movements, their circular form and the principle of homocentricity), the contribution of empiricism is predominant in Eudoxus' work. Its preponderance can be felt, not only in the choice of the more adaptable mechanism made up of spheres, but still more in the absence—surprising in a mathematician—of all mathematical elaboration. Neither speeds of rotation nor angles of inclination of the axes were determined in any other way than by reference to the observed facts. In short, mathematics is brought in solely when it is needed to describe the parts of the sphere: great circle, equator, axis, poles. It probably figured also in another chapter, which our quotation left completely aside, concerned with the relations between the speeds of rotation and the distances of the planets. We shall return to this later. But if we confine ourselves to the structure or the theory of the spheres, we shall discover that in that theory arithmetic and geometry are not required. Let us illustrate this point by considering two different spherical systems, that of the Sun and that of Venus: we shall see that the step from observation to the supposed mechanism is direct.

Solar spheres. The rotation of the first sphere is fixed by its *isochrony* with the revolution of the fixed stars: it completes its own revolution in one sidereal day, turning in the same direction and round the same axis as the sphere of the fixed stars. The rotation of the second sphere is fixed by the observed duration of the solar year: it completes its revolution in 365 days, and so turns at an angular velocity of about one degree per day $\left(\text{to be precise } \dfrac{360°}{365}\right)$, but in the opposite direction to the sphere of the fixed stars and the first sphere, since this degree represents a daily delay of the solar day relative to the sidereal day; while, finally, it turns round the same axis as the circle of the zodiac (or ecliptic), since the Sun travels from one tropic to the other in the course of its revolution. As for the rotation of the third sphere, this is fixed by the variations in latitude observed at the extreme points reached by the Sun at the time of the solstices, and by the fraction of the day (probably estimated as $\frac{1}{8}$) to be added to 365 days in order for the Sun to return to exactly the same point relative to the stars, which in the same period have completed one rotation fewer together with this fraction more. The departure in latitude provides a direct measure of the inclination of the axis of this sphere relative to the ecliptic, while the direction of its rotation is allowed to be the same as that of the preceding sphere, since this fraction of a day is to be added to the one day's delay, and represents a very slow movement relative to that sphere; and, finally, the period of rotation is estimated to be eight years, since (according to a later source) the annual divergence of the Sun relative to the stars amounts to only one-eighth of the circumference of the sphere.

Modern historians have been greatly preoccupied by Eudoxus' teachings about the third sphere. For a long time it was thought that Eudoxus had discovered the phenomenon of the procession of the equinoxes, which advances the equinoxes in time by about fifty seconds each year and so delays the return of the Sun to its initial position by the same amount. But if his instruments had been precise enough to permit the observation of so minute a difference, it would have been clear after eight years that the divergence between the Sun and the stars had increased instead of returning to zero. In fact, it takes some 258 centuries for the equinox to return to the same celestial longitude. The supposed lateral movement of the solsticial points on either side of the tropic circle, on the other hand, is illusion. What then had Eudoxus done? There is only one possible explanation: that his instruments had misled him. Actually, if his observations had revealed to him only the annual delay of the Sun relative to the stars, two spheres would have been enough, with the second completing its backward rotation in $365\frac{1}{8}$ days instead of 365. But he was measuring the Sun's position in latitude using the shadow of a *gnomon*, and he believed that he could discern some slight differences from year to year, and these he quite naturally thought he could relate to the slight delay of the solar year relative to the astral year. It may well be, also, that he did not begin by noticing these differences on the *gnomon*, but rather supposed that the Sun underwent variations in latitude similar to the perfectly authentic ones of the Moon, and subsequently thought that he had discerned these variations in an observation to verify this supposition. However this may be he was convinced that he had seen them, for he notes down in the *Mirror*, after talking about the variations of the Moon, the remark we have already quoted:

The sun also is observed to make a variation in the neighbourhood of the tropics, though this is much less apparent to the eye and is extremely small. (Fr. 63)

The spheres of Venus. When one records on a celestial sphere the positions successively occupied by Venus in the course of its synodic revolution, one finds that its path traces the outline of a saw-tooth. First the planet follows out an arc of a circle from west to east (from O to B on the diagram below), then it moves backwards along a shorter arc (from B to D) and starts off again along a circular arc identical to the first (from D to A'). Its speed meanwhile increases in the middle of each circular arc (at O and Q) and decreases at the extremities of each arc until the planet seems to be stationary (at B and D).

Eudoxus' first sphere accounts for the track that Venus would describe each day if its path involved no irregularities. As with the first spheres of each system, its rotation is accordingly identical in every respect to that of the sphere of the fixed stars: one revolution from east to west per sidereal day. The second sphere displaces this orbit along the ecliptic and explains the slight daily delay of the planet by comparison with the stars: it completes one revolution in 365 days in a direction opposite to the preceding one and around the same axis as the ecliptic.

If the system included only two spheres Venus would simply describe the circle passing through the points OQO' etc. on the above diagram, where its rotation has (so to say) been rolled out on to a plane. The third sphere, as in the case of the Sun, is supposed to explain the deviation in latitude on either side of the ecliptic. Rotating perpendicular to the second sphere, it transforms the west-east path of the planet into a spiral twisted around this path. And as the planet borne along this spiral takes nineteen months to regain its original position relative to the Sun, whose orbit during this time has closely followed the path of the ecliptic, the rotation of the third sphere is assumed to last nineteen months. Finally, the business of the fourth sphere is, on the one hand, to reduce the amplitude of the spiral, whose radius in theory extends to the poles of the universe, so that this amplitude shall equal the divergence of the planet actually observed and, on the other hand, to show the reason for its retrogradation. If this sphere simply turned in the opposite direction to the third, around the same axis and with the same period, the divergence would be cancelled out and the two spheres would be without effect. It is therefore assumed to rotate in another way, which can be defined as follows:

(i) with the same period as the third sphere, so that the resultant of the two rotations shall bring the planet after nineteen months back to the same position relative to the Sun, but

(ii) on an axis whose angle to the axis of the ecliptic is determined by the planet's actually observed divergence in latitude, and

(iii) in the opposite direction to the third sphere, i.e. in the same direction as the first.

The inclination of the axis towards the ecliptic has the effect of reducing the divergence to agree with the observed divergence. On account of this inclination, the rotation in an opposite direction, instead of cancelling out the effect of the third sphere, produces a to-and-fro path whose shape is like a recumbent figure-of-eight, its longer axis coinciding with the great circle projecting on to the fourth sphere by the ecliptic. To this hitherto unknown curve Eudoxus gave the name of 'hippopede': this was the name given by horsemen at that time to the shape which we today call a horse fetter, and which does indeed resemble a figure 8.

Venus traces out the two twists of the hippopede in nineteen months. But as the poles of the third sphere are

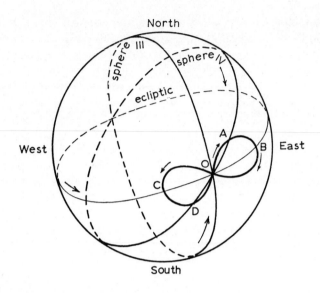

themselves being carried along the ecliptic by the second, completing their circuit in one year, the curve drawn by the planet is stretched out or (so to say) untwisted as it travels through space. So, at the moment when the planet, having set out from the point *O*, might be expected to return there, having in nine and a half months followed out one whole twist of the hippopede, it ends up in fact at the new position of this point, marked *Q* on the previous diagram. Thus arises the saw-tooth track which is so characteristic of the observed motion of Venus. Furthermore, the speeds of the rotation of the second sphere and of the translation of the planet along its path combine to produce accelerations and retardations. Between *D* and *A*, as the planet is moving eastwards in the same direction as the second sphere, their speeds add up and reach a maximum at the point *O*. Between *A* and *B* the actual retrogradation of the planet sets in: the apparent speed diminishes and ends by falling to zero at the point *B*. From *B* to *C*, the retrogradation being more rapid than the forward rotation of the second sphere, the planet starts off again in a westward direction at a speed which reaches a maximum at the point *O*. Thereafter the retrogradation finishes (*C*) and from *D* on the eastward movement slowly takes over, after a moment of immobility.

Modern mathematicians have marvelled not only at the ingenuity of this system, which explains the apparent motions of the planets, but even more at the prodigious mathematical apparatus which (as it seemed to them) Eudoxus had to call into play in order to calculate the hippopede without the help of trigonometry. And indeed, using the methods available to the science of his time, this curve would have to be described as that drawn on the surface of a sphere by a thin cylinder which passes immediately below this surface at the point *O*, or (if we prefer) which is internally tangent to it at this point. Without having to be particularly versed in the analysis of curves, the reader can easily judge the complexity of the equation determined by this specification. So if Eudoxus had really worked out the track of his hippopede on the celestial vault mathematically, his genius would certainly have been past description. Unfortunately, this hypothesis is probably illusory: he did not compute mathematically the curve so described, and was content to reconstruct it empirically, taking his patient observations and the mechanism of enclosed spheres as his starting-point.

If we deprive Eudoxus of the doubtful credit for having achieved a mathematical miracle, he still has enough titles to fame to make many mathematicians envious. The very discovery of the hippopede has a touch of genius about it, for the daily record of the position of Venus—as we must remember—furnished astronomy with a saw-toothed curve. Now no less genius was required to convert these saw-teeth into the hippopede, and to decompose this hippopede into spherical motions than would have been required to represent these motions by the figure of a thin cylinder internally tangent to the sphere. However much reason and the silence of the ancient texts compel us to cut down the mathematical performances of Eudoxus, the analysis of his theory as summarized by Eudemus testifies to his extraordinary deductive capacity. And we must praise no less his outstanding practical talents, remembering that to verify his theory of the planetary movements he was very probably obliged to rotate a celestial globe by hand, as many times as there are days in the period of rotation—or in an important part of the rotation—of a planet, through the four movements which each day determine the position of the heavenly body in question: the complete circuit from east to west, the slight falling back and deviation along the ecliptic, the additional falling back and deviation towards one of the poles, and the final correction of these two elements by nearly contrary motions. And if, strictly speaking, patience alone is needed to carry through such a verification satisfactorily, since it calls only for the marking of some hundreds of points on a globe, both patience and exactitude are required for the subsequent, inverse operation, of plotting on a celestial globe night after night the observed positions of a planet, and then identifying the curve which unites them in a system explicable by the movements of spheres. For Saturn, for instance, a complete record would have demanded nearly 11,000 observations: a partial, but adequate, account calls at the least for one-tenth of this number —and that is still large enough.

Remarkable though they are, the merits we have demonstrated are not astonishing in a great astronomer: indeed, one would be more astonished to find them lacking. But these by no means exhaust the whole genius of Eudoxus, nor —one may say—his individuality. For there is something about his theory which transcends the customary methods of astronomy. This may well need to be described as something more than mere intuition, for that is already broadly covered by his deductive capacity. Alternatively, if we must stick to that term, then we must widen it to embrace that breadth of vision which concerns itself less with the precise links to be followed out in a chain of argument than with the total picture of the elements under consideration. In the case of Eudoxus, however, whose intuition (in this wider sense of the word) was inspired, perhaps without his knowing it, by the secular doctrines of the philosophers, it is perhaps more precise to speak of a *feeling*: the feeling for the totality of the cosmos.

Before summing up, let us pause to consider this last theme. As we saw at the beginning of this chapter, Eudoxus was dominated equally by his preconceived idea of regular, uniform and circular movements and by his desire to respect the facts of observation. His theory almost succeeds in reconciling these two imperatives. But what is more, it reconciles them within the framework of an all-embracing view of the universe, instead of restricting itself to particular theorems. In its aims, if not in its precision, this view is also that of Plato, and before him that of Anaxagoras and of Empedocles. While taking a more detailed look at the world, Eudoxus had no broader view than his predecessors. On one point, however, he had a prophetic vision, which they had never experienced and which fills his work with a quite impressive vitality: this was the vision—2,000 years before Newton and for the first time in history—of a universal law of gravitation. To the first philosophers the universe had seemed to be populated by stars, or by many worlds; some of them had been brave enough to conceive of the infinite; but none before Eudoxus had dared to imagine that the movements which animated it were ruled by an immutable mechanical law. They were content to accept mythological fables, biological explanations which compared the world to a living organism, or even speculations of a moral kind, involving the rhythm of a justice which controlled the alternations of transgression and punishment. Eudoxus is the first to have conceived a mathematical explanation of the manifest regularities in the movements of the heavenly bodies, and this is the only part of astronomy in which he seems to have made use of the resources of mathematics.

How, in fact, did he envisage the spatial arrangement and combined movements of his hollow spheres? A passage from Aristotle, which clearly refers back either to his theory (though without actually naming him) or to a theory directly modelled on his own, tells us first that he located the sphere of the fixed stars at the boundary of the universe, and that he distributed the wandering stars throughout the whole region included between this boundary and the Earth.

As for the arrangement of the heavenly bodies, the relation between their respective speeds and their lesser or greater distance from the Earth, and the distances which separate them one from another, it is necessary to base one's views on astronomical study, which leads to satisfactory results. The proper speed of each body is proportional to its distance from the fixed stars, and that is why some move more quickly and others more slowly. Indeed, given that the rotation of the firmament, at the very boundary of the universe, is the most rapid and involves a single movement, while the movements of the other bodies are slower and involve more numerous movements (remembering that each star rotates in a direction opposite to the rotation of the sky and according to its own orbit), it is reasonable to suppose that the star nearest to the first revolution, which is also the simplest, takes the longest time to follow out its orbit, while the most distant one completes it in the shortest time. And likewise for the other bodies, the nearer taking the longer times to complete their revolutions, and the most distant the shorter times. The nearest, indeed, is most held back by the rotation of the firmament and the most distant least, on account of its remoteness. As for those in the intervening region, their speeds are proportional to their distances, as the mathematicians demonstrate. (*De Caelo*, 291ª29)

The first Greek astronomers had not known how the Sun, Moon and planets were set out in the region between the Earth and the Heavens, but little by little this had been recognized and demonstrated. By Plato's time, he could treat this as a truism, so that in that respect Eudoxus was no innovator. But astronomers and philosophers up to Plato, guided by the idea that the universe must combine all sort of perfections, had concluded that the inter-planetary distances must express themselves through symmetries of aesthetic relations, or else through numbers possessing some special virtues. Plato himself, following the example of certain Pythagoreans, would have the planetary circles spaced according to the proportions of the arithmetic, geometric and harmonic means: it could not be the case

(he thought) that the cosmos was not ruled by harmony—
was not the image of the most perfect of perfections. How
do Eudoxus' views compare with these? The evidence
quoted here shows that he put forward an astonishingly
modern conception, according to which the inter-planetary
distances were linked to the period of revolution of the
heavenly bodies, which were themselves subject to the
influence of the all-powerful rotation of the sphere of the
fixed stars. How should one think of this influence? Eudoxus'
theory supposes in principle that the exterior sphere of each
system reproduces exactly the rotation of the sphere of the
fixed stars. But since, apart from the one furthest away from
the Earth, these systems are separated from the sphere of the
fixed stars by several spheres rotating around axes other
than that of the universe, it is impossible for the external
movement to be transmitted by way of a central axis.
Evidently, then, the vast mechanism thought of by Eudoxus
was conceived by him as lacking all material substance, the
axes of his spheres being in his eyes as immaterial as the
spheres themselves. He must accordingly have thought of
the whole universe as traversed by forces which maintained
each system on an ideal axis, so transmitting the rotation of
the sphere of the fixed stars to the outer spheres of all the
planetary systems. And, within each complex, he must
have imagined other forces, governed by principles unknown
to us, holding the idealized spheres on unreal axes and con-
ferring on these axes the necessary movements. Thus spheres,
axes and poles played parts in his vision of the cosmic movements very like those we assign to the centres and radii of
the ecliptical orbits pursued by the planets and their satellites.
In other words (we may say) he saw them only as geometrical
notions, as does modern astronomy, with this single difference, that his figures move while our ellipses remain
stationary. Eudoxus thus broke entirely with the materialistic
concepts of Greek astronomy, well illustrated as late as
Plato's *Timaeus*, e.g. in such passages as the following:

> Next he cleft the structure so formed lengthwise into two
> halves and, laying them across one another, middle

163

upon middle in the shape of the letter X, he bent them in a circle and joined them, making them meet themselves and each other at a point opposite to that of their original contact: and he comprehended them in that motion which revolves uniformly and in the same place, and one of the circles he made exterior and one interior. (36 BC)

Such is his vision of the movements and of their transmission. Yet how did he conceive of the forces responsible for these movements? In modern astronomy, the orbit of a planet may be defined very simply as the geometrical locus of the points where the effects of the contrary forces—centrifugal and centripetal—balance out. Eudoxus was not yet in any position to envisage the principle of gravitation so simply. But he appears already to have had some obscure intuition of an equilibrium between contrary forces. Being fixed relative to the axis of the universe, all the outer spheres of the seven planetary mechanisms are carried round by this axis in the rotation of the fixed stars, and this demands no further attractive force: in this case, the transmission of the force is purely mechanical. But Aristotle testifies that, by virtue of some principle which he does not state, each of these spheres exerts on the counter-rotation of the spheres it encloses a braking influence which cannot be explained by any mechanical combination. Moreover, he tells us that this effect falls off according to the distance separating the planetary complex from the sphere of the fixed stars, as though, while maintaining the speed transmitted to it by the axis of the universe, each outer sphere lost with increasing distance some part of the force associated with its movement. So Eudoxus must have supposed that the *linear speed* of each outer sphere, which effectively decreases in proportion to the radius of the sphere, is connected with its braking force.

To sum up: with an inspired intuition he had foreseen that the movement of each planet along the orbit imposed on it by the layout of the spheres is governed by two invariable and opposed forces: the force produced by the westerly rotation of the sphere of the fixed stars, and that produced by the easterly rotation of the sphere whose axis is fixed relative to the ecliptic. His error sprang from not knowing that these forces originate in the attraction and repulsion of the bodies themselves, and from having associated them with the speeds of the rotary movements. One can the more readily excuse him for this, seeing that his ignorance did not prevent him from making the periods of the planetary revolutions (quite correctly) dependent on the forces producing them, and not on the lengths of the orbits to be travelled. He proved his astonishing perspicacity also in asserting that these forces are proportional to the distances separating their point of origin from their different points of application: in concerning himself with the attractive force defined by the law of universal gravitation, a modern astronomer might speak of the revolutions of the planets in very similar terms. So it is no exaggeration to regard the astronomy of Eudoxus as a remote forerunner of modern astronomy, even though it did not subsequently develop in the direction of Kepler and Galileo.

This last glance at the most original, and at the same time the least familiar aspects of the theory of the spheres leads us into the mathematical part of Eudoxus' astronomy. And the application of the laws of proportionality to the speeds of the 'wandering stars' does indeed involve the general theory of proportions. It may even perhaps represent the precise goal towards which this theory was directed. By calling as witnesses Archimedes, who credits Eudoxus with the assertion that the diameter of the Sun is nine times greater than that of the Earth, and also Aristotle, who calculates that the terrestrial circumference is 400,000 stades (47,250 miles), and by accepting finally an estimate assumed by Aristarchus of Samos about 280 B.C., according to which the diameter of the Sun would enter roughly 720 times into the circumference of the sphere of the fixed stars, a patient mathematician could work out—to a satisfactory approximation—the distances allotted by Eudoxus to each of the 'wandering stars', bearing in mind their observed periods of revolution. Part of his treatise *On Speeds* was probably devoted to these calculations.

Conclusion

We have said enough to show the place occupied by the theory of the spheres in the mathematics of Eudoxus: it is time to bring an already long chapter to a close. Before leaving the astronomer of Cnidus, the reader will be grateful for one final glance at the picture of him passed down by antiquity. We must first recall the brilliant teacher at Cyzicus or the lecturer at Athens, surrounded by a constellation of pupils several of whom were to carry on his work: for example, Menaechmus and Dinostratus in geometry, and Polemarchus and Callippus in astronomy. Into this portrait, perhaps rather traditional, can be woven some other, more authentic, traits of character. First of all there are his curiosity and taste for travel, which lead him as far as Egypt and which, in his monumental seven-volume geography, the *Circuit of the Earth*, display themselves through a style worthy at times of Marco Polo and through a multitude of reports about strange things of all kinds: the flooding of the Nile, underwater springs, the strange customs of the Massagetes and so on. Further, there are his worldly inclinations, which caused him to be singled out by the King of Sparta and chosen as a diplomatic courier to the Pharaoh, which won him his long residence with the priests of Heliopolis, which assured him the protection of the satrap Mausolus, and which, finally, resulted in his being called back to his native city as legislator and rewarded by an honorific inscription. These very characteristic features led some of his biographers to include him among the Sophists, and so to emphasize, in his literary portrait, the two distinctive traits of his line of great teachers: persuasive eloquence and a taste for money. Such is the rather unexpected memory of him preserved by most ancient writers.

While recognizing how far this was a result of the habit common among Greek biographers, of classifying individual characters in preconceived and schematic categories, we can scarcely dismiss this testimony entirely, however disappointing it may be at first glance. To be a mathematician of Eudoxus' kind is not necessarily inconsistent with having a personality of the type Jung calls 'extrovert'. Does that mean that this characterization describes his personality exhaustively? Certainly not. Quoting from him a thesis about the supremacy of pleasure in beings animated by greed and lust, Aristotle praises him in terms which strike a very different tone:

> His arguments about pleasure carried conviction more on account of the perfection of his character than through their contents. Eudoxus passed, indeed, for a man of remarkable moderation. Again he did not seem to embrace these arguments as being a friend of pleasure, but because he regarded them as conforming to the truth. (*Eth. Nicom.* 1172ᵇ9)

Coming from a philosopher who had known Eudoxus personally, this evidence by itself is worth more than all the gossip of antiquity. What then does it teach us?—that the lively features of the lecturer eager to convince his public overlaid an unemotional and rigorous scientific conscience; that the artifices of style were the tools of a mind which loved truth alone; that, despite all his qualities as a forceful speaker, Eudoxus dedicated the best of himself to science rather than to the furtherance of his career. Although less emphasized by his biographers, this preference did not however escape them, and they did not hesitate to associate it with his vocation as an astronomer. One of them paints a picture of him as being so captivated by his observations of the shape and size of the Sun that he would beg the day-star to consume him, like Phaeton, with the heat of its flames. Another makes much of his renunciation of material things, as implying a life devoted entirely to contemplation, and imagines Eudoxus retiring to the summit of a high mountain, to end his days meditating on the movements of the stars. These eloquent passages owe no doubt more to a moralist's vision of the ideal astronomer than to the historical facts. Still, it is precisely in Eudoxus' time that the very word for contemplation—*theoria*—enters the philosophers' vocabulary, lending all its moral and metaphysical weight to the ideal of a contemplative life, as contrasted with the political life, practical life, or life given over to pleasure. Now the philosophers knowingly borrowed this term from astronomy, as being *par excellence* the science of contemplation. But it had not always been so, and of all the astronomers of antiquity Eudoxus is the one who succeeded in making it so.

Is it legitimate to carry the hypothesis further, and to infer from these coincidences that philosophy took Eudoxus as its model of the man for whom patient observation led to knowledge? History does not authorize this, yet it does make it worth while to consider in conjunction the impulse given to astronomy by Eudoxus and the simultaneous working-out of the doctrine of the contemplative life. About 350, shortly after Eudoxus had published his most important discoveries, Heraclides of Pontus, himself the author of a revolutionary cosmography, puts into the mouth of Pythagoras (in his capacity as the prince of philosophers) the maxim:

Man is born to contemplate the sky.[1]

Let us imagine for a moment with what intensity Eudoxus must have given himself over to his thoughts when he equipped the starry space of night with twenty-seven immense spheres and, watching the slow rise of the stars, followed out their majestic rotations. Then at last we can realize that the philosophers had glimpsed, for the time being at any rate, the possibility of raising oneself with the help of astronomy to a contemplation of the supreme truths: they were to forget about it a few years later. Whether in some nocturnal lesson they had in truth explored the horizons of the sky under the guidance of Eudoxus, or whether they had only dreamed of such an exploration, according to him they were haunted by the vision which inspired them to the new ideal of the contemplative life. Even if we could recognize no other effects of the modern style with which he stamped astronomy, this one reflection alone is enough to display the singular vigour of his influence.

1. The quotation is taken from a passage in Iamblichus' *Life of Pythagoras* (Chap. 58 ff.). But Iamblichus is himself drawing on an account which Cicero derives explicitly from Heraclides, in an abbreviated form omitting this quotation, in the *Tusculans*, V, 3,8.

VI

Harmony

However far back one goes in the history of Greece, the education of the young seems always to have been founded on two branches of instruction alone: gymnastics and music. Instruction in gymnastics and physical training served in the beginning as a preparation for war. Music comprised a solid training in singing and dancing, as well as an introduction to the playing of the lyre as an accompaniment to singing. This had, above all, the practical aim of providing the cities with the choirs needed for the religious festivals. From the eighth century B.C. on, so as to maintain the enthusiasm of teachers and pupils by an official recognition of their efforts, some of the cities instituted regular contests in these two fields of study. The Olympic Games are the best-known example, among a score of others.

From the fifth century, with the appearance of new forms of teaching which were beginning to compete with the traditional education, the defenders of gymnastics and music found themselves compelled more and more to justify their position both to their critics and competitors and to a hesitant public. Thus there appeared for the first time pedagogical arguments intended to displace the appeals to public utility with which the archaic period had been content. In the case of gymnastics there was less insistence on the development of physical strength and more on the better direction of energy through the discipline of training and the pursuit of a virile bearing. The perfection of the statues of heroes and athletes was held out as a model for adolescents. As for music: much was said about the value of singing in the formation of character, especially that of religious chants and war-songs, but in addition there were the first attempts to state in the form of convincing arguments an as yet confused impression of a musical order capable of disciplining the pupil's soul and developing the cardinal virtues. The mathematical science of harmony was worked out in just this situation. Its aim, at least at the start, was to grasp in rational terms the order of which musical feeling was a presentiment.

The very word harmony had been used by the Greeks in several senses, some of them having nothing to do with music. The link between these senses and common usage was the general and fundamental conception of *arrangement* or *adjustment*. In music, the word referred primarily to the *fixing* of the strings to the yoke of the lyre, but we are familiar with it above all in the transferred meanings of *scale* or *concord*— that is, of *harmony* in the modern sense of the term. As a result, the science bearing this name was aimed directly towards those aspects of music which seemed to involve some principle of order and of organization, i.e. specifically towards the scale and concord after which it was named. The first attempts at grasping the musical order in intelligible terms apparently concerned themselves with rhythm: there was a mathematical rhythm before there was a harmony. For rhythm is the basis of dance, and its order can be recognized more easily in the pattern of steps than can the order of harmony in the sound-pattern of tunes. Thus, from 450 B.C. on, there was an accepted code of rhythms which gave birth, a good century later, to Aristoxenus of Tarentum's mathematical theory of rhythm.

Without doubt, harmony as a science was born from the technical study of the scale. Up to the end of the sixth century the tuning of the lyre was subject to no generally accepted rules. Each city imposed its national melodies on its musicians, and these men had to adjust their instruments so as to accompany them most suitably. The scales worked out from these data differed considerably from city to city. Little by little, however, practical experience led to simplifications, particularly from the time when poets of international fame began to be called on to display their talents for the amusement of audiences foreign to their native towns. To one of these men, Lasos of Hermione, better known as a theoretician than as a musician, is attributed the first treatise attempting to set out, region by region, the different characteristic ways of tuning the lyre. His literary activity is dated around 510, at which time we can say with confidence that, whatever the reliability of the reports about Lasos, the number of Greek scales was diminishing and certain sequences of intervals were becoming common to all. From this time on, these intervals were recognized as constituting the framework of the musical scale, and received in turn the name of *harmony*. They were the tone, the fourth, the fifth and the octave, and were set out on four of the seven cords of the lyre in such a way as to form the arpeggio represented in modern notation as *do—fa—sol—do*, or rather, descending according to Greek custom from higher-pitched to lower, as *do—sol—fa—do*. The other cords of the lyre, three or in some cases more, were allotted either to intermediate notes, or occasionally to notes outside the octave. Their tension was free to vary between certain limits, and the different permitted combinations gave the different national scales regularized by the system of Lasos, the so-called *modes*: the dorian mode, the phrygian mode, the lydian mode, etc.

During the fifth century the regularization of the scales became still more marked, while at the same time the use of intervals smaller than the tone—semi-tone, quarter-tone, or intermediate intervals—began to be codified. But the harmony of the four fundamental intervals remained untouched, and it was there that the theoreticians were to discern the principle of musical order. Their mathematical analysis is based on a numerical translation of those intervals whose working-out is hard to date. Perhaps technical problems arising in the manufacture of musical instruments first demonstrated the possibility of solutions in numerical terms. The separation between the holes to be drilled in a reed when making a flute, for instance, had probably been

determined as early as the sixth century by a simple calculation of proportions. According to the traditions of antiquity,
the discovery of the numerical relations corresponding to the
different intervals went back to Lasos himself, who is said to
have measured them by the following procedure:

> Using vases, he would have studied the greater and
> lesser speed of the movements which give rise to the con-
> cords. Then, reckoning that the relations between the
> concords are expressible as numbers, he demonstrated
> this using the vases. Having taken several vases of the
> same volume and shape, he left one of them empty and
> half filled another with a liquid, then struck them in
> turn and so obtained the concord of the octave. Again
> leaving one vase empty, and filling the other a quarter
> full, he obtained on striking them the concord of the
> fourth. Finally, for the fifth, he filled one vase a third
> full. The ratio of the empty volumes was thus 2 to 1 for
> the octave, 3 to 2 for the fifth, and 4 to 3 for the fourth.
> [Quoted by Theon of Smyrna, p. 59 Hiller]

The experiment here described is suspect for two reasons.
To begin with, it is clear that the emptier the vase, the lower
the note. In order to correspond to the empty volumes, the
ratios quoted should thus be reversed: the high note is to the
bass as 1 is to 2, or 2 to 3, or 3 to 4. In the second place, the
laws of acoustics demonstrate that intervals measured in this
way are to be expressed by the squares of the required ratios.
One must accordingly concede that this account does not
correspond to historical reality, and even that it is wholly
fictitious. But it makes use of the correct ratios and of a theory
of sound already familiar to the physicist of the fifth century,
and to Plato, in which are related the notions of volume and
sound, movement and speed. Thus, without committing oneself to the view that these experiments led to the first exact
measurement of these ratios, one must recognize that they
had already been determined by the time—towards the
end of fifth century—when the mathematicians became
aware of their interest, and, in order to study them, founded a
new science: harmony.

The names of the mathematicians concerned are not known

to us. It is, however, probable that they belonged to the Pythagorean circle of southern Italy. Here is how Archytas of Tarentum, several decades later, at the beginning of his *Harmony*, places their work in the hierarchy of the mathematical sciences and describes its experimental phase:

The mathematicians seem to me to have arrived at correct conclusions, and it is not therefore surprising that they have a true conception of the nature of each individual thing; for, having reached such correct conclusions regarding the nature of the universe, they were bound to see in its true light the nature of particular things as well. Thus they have handed down to us clear knowledge about the speed of the stars, their risings and settings, and about geometry, arithmetic, and sphaeric, and last, not least, about music: for these sciences seem to be sisters, since the two primitive aspects of reality to which they apply [that is to say, number and magnitude] are sisters.

They believed, first of all, that there could be no noise without a previous impact of one body against another. They declared that there is a shock (impact) when two movable objects meet and collide. When moving in contrary directions, these movable objects produce a noise by their very meetings: but, when moving in the same direction at unequal speeds, they also produce a noise through the shock which results when one overtakes the other. Some of these noises cannot be perceived by our nature, either because of the weakness of the shock or because of its distance away from us, or again because the shock is of too great a force, for shocks which are too strong do not penetrate our ears any more than too broad a stream of liquid can be poured into a receptacle with too narrow a neck.

Of the noises that excite our senses, some appear shrill: these are the ones which travel rapidly to us from the place where the shock is produced. Others sound low—these are the ones which travel to us slowly and weakly. Thus, if one takes a stick and shakes it to and fro slowly and weakly, it emits a deep tone from the resulting shock. When, on the contrary, it is brandished quickly and strongly, it emits a shrill sound. And this is not the only experiment which teaches us, but there is also another: if we want to produce a strong, shrill sound when talking or singing, we achieve this by giving to the voice a large amount of breath. And likewise for missiles: those which are thrown forcibly travel a long way, while those which are thrown weakly fall nearby, for the air yields more easily to that which is moving strongly while it yields less easily to that which is moving feebly.

It will be the same, accordingly, for the sounds of the voice: that which is set in motion by a powerful breath will be strong and shrill, that which is set in motion by a weak breath will be low and slight. We can convince ourselves of this once again by the following very convincing proof, that one and the same man, if he speaks in a high voice, can make himself heard afar, but, if he speaks in a low voice, he is unable to make himself heard even nearby. And again, the breath expelled by the mouth into the pipes of a flute, if it escapes through the holes near the mouth, produces by its force a shriller sound, but if it escapes through the more distant holes, it produces a deeper sound. It is thus evident that rapid movement produces a shrill sound, slow movement a deep sound. . . . And when one blocks the lower end of a straw and blows, it emits a deep sound. But if one blows down half or any other fraction of the straw, it emits a shrill sound. For the same breath displaces itself weakly in a long volume and strongly in a short volume. . . . From the evidence of these numerous examples, it accordingly follows that high sounds move themselves more quickly and deep sounds more slowly. (*Vorsokr.* 47 B 1)

Basing themselves on that conclusion, which seemed to them duly established after experiments that were doubtless less varied than those that Archytas puts forward, the mathematicians had determined the mathematical ratios corresponding to the intervals of the whole-tone $\left(\dfrac{9}{8}\right)$, the fourth $\left(\dfrac{4}{3}\right)$, the fifth $\left(\dfrac{3}{2}\right)$ and the octave $\left(\dfrac{2}{1}\right)$. They had likewise adopted the usage of expressing the absolute value of the notes corresponding to these intervals by the first whole-numbers satisfying their ratios, namely, in the order *do—fa—sol—do*, the numbers 6, 8, 9 and 12. The opening of the quotation suggests that, in these numbers, they believed that they grasped the reality of sound, but they do not seem to have pursued the mathematical analysis much further. The calculation of the mathematical ratios corresponding to other intervals, and the discovery of the inherent properties of the ratios they had already determined certainly date from the time of Archytas. They constituted the chief subject-matter of his *Harmony*.

Archytas

One of Archytas' first concerns was to determine mathematically the intervals less than a tone. Musicians had actually been using for a long time not only the semi-tone, which is in a certain sense contained in the fourth and fifth, but also intermediate shades between the tone and the semitone, or even smaller than the semi-tone, such as the quartertone. The classification of these shades into those of *diatonic* type—where, in the fundamental tetracord, the semi-tone is not heard as a divided tone (*mi—fa—sol—la*)—those of *chromatic* type—where the half-tone, replaced at times by adjacent intervals, is heard as the fraction of a whole-tone (*mi—fa—fa♯—la*)—and those of *enharmonic* type—where the semi-tone is itself sub-divided into quarter-tone intervals (*mi—mi⁺—fa—la*)—is introduced at the time of Archytas as an attempt to codify these shades empirically so as to put a brake on the anarchical tendencies of musical practice. Its main effect was to spread the idea (very questionable, but at that time unquestioned) that these small intervals served as units of measurement for the scale, as the foot is a unit of length or the dram a unit of weight. The school of the *Harmonists*, which made itself much talked about, advocated the use of the quarter-tone because they considered it the smallest interval still perceptible to a trained ear; on this basis they proposed a very simple system of scales which musicians whom they taught should be able to execute on their instruments without any trouble. The researches that

Archytas inaugurated on the mathematical level thus had their place in the actual practice of music, and answered a need. At the same time, they were to demonstrate the incommensurability of the audible fractions of the whole-tone, and thereby to condemn in principle even those empirical solutions which the supporters of the different harmonic types had advocated.

In order first of all to determine the range of the semi-tone, Archytas proceeds to reduce the interval of the fourth by two successive whole-tones. Expressed in terms of mathematical operations, this subtraction is equivalent to two successive divisions of the interval of the fourth by the interval of a tone:

$$\frac{4}{3} : \frac{9}{8} : \frac{9}{8} = \frac{256}{243}$$

Now if, by a fresh division, this fraction is itself subtracted from a whole-tone, we obtain in place of the same semi-tone a slightly larger interval:

$$\frac{9}{8} : \frac{256}{243} = \frac{2187}{2048}$$

Archytas thus proved that the semi-tone of the perfect fourth is not strictly equal to half the perfect whole-tone. This being so, it followed that mathematics contradicted not only the testimony of the ear, which believes that it hears a perfect semi-tone, but also reality itself, seeing that this perfect semi-tone had been assumed to have a real existence.

How was one to react to this tiresome evidence? So far as practical music was concerned, it was easy to make up perfect fourths from unequal intervals whose inequality would be imperceptible. Thus Archytas proposes for the diatonic tetracord *mi—fa—sol—la* the fractions $\frac{28}{27}$, $\frac{8}{7}$, $\frac{9}{8}$, whose product is in fact $\frac{4}{3}$, and approximatory sequences of the same kind for the chromatic and enharmonic tetracords. But these practical solutions left untouched the problem of the relation between mathematics and reality. It was necessary to face it directly—and mathematically. This part of Archytas's researches has been preserved for us, along with so many other chapters in ancient mathematics, by a treatise of Euclid whose original title was *Elements of Music*, and of which a severely abridged version has come down to us under the name of the *Section of the Canon*—the *canon* being a single-stringed instrument designed for acoustic measurements.

The first theorem of this treatise establishes the notion of the unit of measurement. It may perhaps seem surprising that this should need defining, but it must be remembered that Archytas knew neither of Theaetetus' work on incommensurability, nor—for even more obvious reasons—of Eudoxus' work on proportions. Moreover, Archytas was not dealing with the notion of measure or commensurability in general, but only with the measure of the sonic intervals.

If a multiple interval, on being doubled, produces another interval, this new interval is likewise multiple. (*Sect. can.* 1)

By a *multiple interval*, as opposed to an *epimore interval*, Archytas means one which is expressed by a fraction whose numerator is a multiple of the denominator: e.g. the octave $\left(\dfrac{2}{1}\right)$. The *epimore* interval is represented by fractions of the type

$\dfrac{n+{}^{n}/a}{n}$, where n and a are both whole numbers: e.g. the upper fourth of the tetracord, namely, *sol—do* $\left(\dfrac{12}{9} = \dfrac{9+9/3}{9}\right)$. The

theorem is easily demonstrated: one proves in succession that the first multiple interval is *measured* by its lower note, and then that the second interval (consisting of a higher note *measured* by a lower note, which is itself *measured* by its own lower note) is in its turn multiple. Archytas was certainly thinking here of the double octave $\left(\dfrac{24}{12}\right)$, which is a multiple

of the octave $\left(\dfrac{12}{6}\right)$, whose higher note (12) is itself double the

lower note (6).

The next theorem is the reciprocal of the first:

> If an interval, on being doubled, produces a multiple interval, it is itself multiple. (*Sect. can.* 2)

This theorem can be deduced from the preceding one. But the proof actually surviving proceeds differently. It goes back to a theorem in arithmetic which Archytas knew from Hippocrates of Chios' *Elements*, and which passed from there into Euclid with certain editorial changes:

> If as many numbers as we please be in continued proportion, and the first measures the last, the first will also measure the intermediate numbers. (Cf. Eucl. *Elem.* VIII, Prop. 7)

There follows a theorem to similar effect for *epimore* intervals.

> An epimore interval has no half, and we cannot intercalate in continued proportion either a single number or several numbers. (*Sect. can.* 3)

Let us reduce an epimore interval, e.g. the fifth $\left(\dfrac{12}{9}\right)$,

to its lowest numerical terms $\left(\text{here } \dfrac{4}{3}\right)$; the difference between the numerator and the denominator will always be 1. It follows that two numbers which form an epimore interval are prime to one another. But the terms of a continued proportion (i.e. a geometrical progression) are never prime to one another. So these two numbers are not two terms of a continued proportion.

By this third theorem, Archytas showed that there is no such thing as a mathematical semi-tone, still less a quarter-tone. The theorems which follow are concerned above all with the different possible combinations of intervals. Some bring to light new contradictions between the realities of appearance and those of mathematics, for instance, theorem 9, which proves that the sum of six whole-tones is greater than an octave. Others, by contrast, show how exact are the correspondences supposed to unite the two orders of reality. Such, for instance, are theorems 6 and 7. Theorem 6 proves that the octave $\left(\frac{2}{1}\right)$ is the mathematical product of the fourth $\left(\frac{4}{3}\right)$ and the fifth $\left(\frac{3}{2}\right)$. Theorem 7 proves that the tone $\left(\frac{9}{8}\right)$ is the mathematical quotient of the fourth $\left(\frac{4}{3}\right)$ and the fifth $\left(\frac{3}{2}\right)$. Finally, other theorems deal with intervals which are neither multiple nor epimore. There is the case, for example, with theorem 4, which is concerned with intervals double the fifth, the fourth and the tone. After the exposition of the general theorems summed up here, there follows a detailed analysis of the intervals of the scale.

Although neither theorems and proofs leave the field of mathematics, one can easily divine the conclusions towards which this wholly theoretical analysis was leading. For Archytas it was a matter of showing that the basic intervals of the concord alone unite the two realms, of appearance and of numbers, that they alone are either multiple or epimore, and finally that they alone produce a consonance, while other intervals are neither mathematically exact, nor multiple or epimore, nor—to end with—consonant. An echo of this development is preserved in the *Problems* traditionally attributed to Aristotle:

> Why are neither a double fifth, nor a double fourth consonant, while a double octave is consonant? This is because their extreme notes are not in ratio one to the other, being neither epimores nor multiples. (*Probl.* 41)

In thus distinguishing between consonant and dissonant intervals, Archytas was able to prove that only 'harmony' (i.e. the basic tetracord), being made up of the sole consonant intervals, reveals the mathematical order of the universe. This entrance to the cosmos was one which Plato found particularly seductive. On a strictly mathematical plane, the effect of Archytas' theorems was to exclude from the field of harmony all intervals other than the tone, the fourth, the fifth, the octave and certain combinations larger than the octave. From then on, mathematicians were compelled to concentrate on the basic intervals, which were alone convertible into numerical expressions. Their intrinsic properties having been analysed and defined in the first part of the theory, it remained to study their interrelations. And there Archytas made his greatest discovery—the means.

The Means

The theory of means, whose later development as regards arithmetic was explained above, had its birthplace in harmony. It sprang, indeed, from a consideration of the numerical sequences 6/8/12 (fourth + fifth) and 6/9/12 (fifth + fourth), which are those of the basic intervals of the scale. Analysing the mathematical relations involved in these two sequences, one can quickly see that the second has for its medial number the arithmetic mean of the extreme numbers. In this characteristic resides the special relationship uniting these three numbers. Hence the name *mean*, which refers both to the sequence of three numbers and to their specific relationship: in this case, the mean is known as *arithmetic*.

The relationship of the mean uniting the numbers of the first sequence is less obvious, at any rate to our eyes. In order to recognize it, we must analyse the sequence as Archytas did in the case of the notion of an 'epimore' interval—expressed by a fraction, whose numerator is the sum of the denominator together with a fraction of itself $\left(\frac{n + {}^n/a}{n} \right)$. This interval actually assumes the specific relationship uniting the three numbers of the sequence in question: the fraction $\frac{8}{6}$ bears the same relation to the fraction $\frac{12}{8}$ as an epimore fraction does to that which could be called its 'anti-epimore'. In other words, if 8 is the medial number, it is evident that the difference between 6 and 8 and that between 8 and 12 represent *like fractions*—viz. one-third—of the extreme numbers 6 and 12. When we subtract from 12 one-third of itself and when we add to 6 one-third of itself we obtain 8 in both cases. To this mean Archytas gave the name of *harmonic mean*, as being one characteristic of the harmony of the fourth and the fifth.

Finally, considering now sequences of the types 9/12/16 and 8.12.18 (introduced in theorem 7 of the *Section of the Canon*) which express respectively a sequence of two fourths and two fifths either side of the upper note of the octave (12), Archytas identifies the medial number as being the *geometric* mean between 9 and 16, or between 8 and 18:

$$\frac{16}{12} = \frac{12}{9} \text{ and } \frac{18}{12} = \frac{12}{8}$$

This mean has something geometrical about it, in that the rectangles constructed from the numbers it unites—here 9×12 and 12×16, or 8×12 and 12×18—are similar.

In closing this examination of the relationships embodied in the succession of harmonic intervals, Archytas presents his conclusion in a legitimate tone of satisfaction, which Plato and, after him, Aristotle were soon to echo:

There are accordingly three means in music. The first is arithmetic, the second geometric, and the third is the subcontrary which is known as harmonic. There is an arithmetic mean when three notes differ in the following way: by the same amount that the first exceeds the second, the second exceeds the third. In this relationship, the interval between the notes of greatest value is found to be smallest, while the interval between the notes of smallest value is the greatest. There is a geometric mean when the first note bears to the second the same ratio that the second bears to the third. In this case, the notes of greatest value and those of smallest value produce the same intervals. There is a subcontrary mean (which we call 'harmonic') on the following conditions: by whatever part of itself the first note exceeds the second, the middle note exceeds the third by the same part of the third. In this relationship, the interval between the notes of greatest value is the greatest, that between the notes of the smallest value is the smallest. (*Vorsokr.* 47 B 2)

The discovery of these three means fully justified Archytas' contentment. Indeed, it sealed an indissoluble alliance between reality and number, and appeared to demonstrate past refutation that all the notable aspects of physical reality are governed by mathematics. For the first time, it provided an objective proof that the ontological mathematics inaugurated by the Pythagoreans some ten years earlier was not entirely illusory. We must keep it in mind that, in presenting his sequence of theorems and proofs, Archytas never lost sight of these philosophical consequences. Only if judged by this criterion will the true nature of his researches be appreciated. Although in some of his steps he seems to be looking to the future (e.g. when he experiments with combinations of intervals so as to discover their properties) his theory always came back in the end to the analysis of sensible reality. Anticipating Speusippus in his application of the principle that mathematics should discover and reveal things but not invent them, Archytas aspired only to bring hidden truths to light, not to establish uncertain truths or to proclaim new ones.

These considerations are above all true in the case of the means, even though these very means represent his most original discovery. If, *mutatis mutandis*, one compares his theory with Eudoxus' theory of proportion, one will see that the purpose of Archytas' theorems is to sort out from the whole mass of musical numbers those which make up interesting series, whose relationships one has to distinguish without the help of theorems, while Eudoxus begins by working out a method of demonstration adapted to the study of proportions and goes on to apply this method to all imaginable combinations of proportional terms with the aim of inferring from these combinations themselves some new truths about the concept of proportion. One can remark also that Archytas discovers the means but does not give a demonstration of their properties, while Eudoxus is interested less in discovering new relationships—these of proportion suffice for him—than in demonstrating the properties of the relationships under examination. Moreover, Archytas, like Plato after him, envisaged no other goal for mathematical research than the knowledge of reality, as the sentence with which the first paragraph of his treatise concludes expressly declares:

> The mathematical sciences are concerned with the two primitive appearances [aspects] of reality.

From Archytas to Aristoxenus

We have seen in the chapter on arithmetic how Eudoxus, approaching Archytas' means from the direction of axiomatic mathematics, not only incorporated them entirely into arithmetic but also added three new means (p. 59). There is no room here to return to this subject, and we must rather pay attention to subsequent developments in the science of harmony.

Did harmony pass through an axiomatic phase, like the other mathematical sciences? The fact is, that we know almost nothing about the phase of its history in which, definitions and assumptions being taken as a foundation, a complete theory of sound would have been constructed upon this. We know just enough to answer the question in the affirmative. The testimony of Aristoxenus of Tarentum, to whom we shall return, puts us on the trail of mathematicians who have attempted this approach:

> Some of our predecessors introduced extraneous reasoning and, rejecting the senses as inaccurate fabricated mental principles, asserted that height and depth of pitch consist in certain numerical ratios and relative rates of vibration—a theory utterly extraneous to the subject and quite at variance with the phenomena. (*Harm. Elem.* II, p. 32)

The theorists of harmony whom Aristoxenus here criticizes so harshly, certainly derived from Platonism their conviction that variations in pitch depend on non-material causes, governed by the laws of arithmetic. One could without error locate them within the sphere of influence of the Academy, perhaps at the period when it professed the doctrine summarized by the author of the *Epinomis* as follows:

It is clear that everything which is ordered by music necessarily partakes of rhythm, and of sounds measured by numbers. (978 A)

The mistake of which Aristoxenus accuses these mathematicians is probably this: that, as the principle of their calculations, they had taken a small interval which, when suitably multiplied, was supposed to yield numbers capable of measuring the different intervals. Actually, it is conceivable in theory that a scale might be composed on this principle, whose deviations from the well-tempered scale (either ancient or modern) remained imperceptible to the ear. The inconvenience of such a system was, however, that it involved one almost necessarily in the use of irrational numbers, and that, in any case, the fractions representing the chosen intervals could not be produced exactly, either by instruments or by the voice. The minimum interval, called the *diesis*, was below the limit of perception. It had, declared Aristotle, only a theoretical existence:

The unit of measurement is not always counted in isolation, but sometimes also by its multiples. So it is with the *diesis*, which is counted in pairs, while these pairs are not defined by hearing but by calculation. (*Metaph.* 1053ª14)

Harmony thus developed as astronomy would have done if the mathematicians had conceived of the circular, uniform and regular motions without taking any account of the observed phenomena. The theorists of the scale had postulated the existence of a unit-interval, then defined this unit mathematically by a fraction, and finally constructed—or rather reconstructed—the different Greek scales by a series of multiplications, intended to lead them in the end of a harmonic system which resembled the traditional system acoustically, if not mathematically. Their conception of harmony was thus concerned with an axiomatic system of mathematics, as far as is possible for a mathematical science applied to reality. The erroneous principle that Aristoxenus justly denounced in their work was less an excessively rigorous application of the laws of arithmetic, than the wish to build up from the axioms (from what he calls '*intellectual* causes') the relations between actual sounds, whereas these relations result rather from *sensible* causes.

Is there then a science of harmony which, while belonging to mathematics, at the same time takes suitable account of sensory experiences? Aristoxenus thought that this was so, and his work on musical theory was intended to prove this. With him, this science enters the third and last phase of its evolution: at last it lays claim on behalf of harmony to the principles which Eudoxus had applied to astronomy twenty years earlier.

Let us pause for a minute to consider this author, who played so important a part in the history of music. Aristoxenus, the great musical theorist of the fourth century, was born at Tarentum about 375. Educated in the local Pythagorean tradition by a certain Spintharos, who was perhaps his father, he was certainly influenced by the teachings of Archytas, whose biography he was later to write. He practised his profession of master musician first at Mantinea, the capital of Arcadia, then went down to Corinth, before finally joining the school of the Lyceum which Aristotle opened at Athens in 336. There he trained himself in philosophy, but historical studies mainly preoccupied him and took the chief place in his work as a writer, alongside his works on musical theory. Of all that he wrote—453 books— there survive today only vestiges of some twenty treatises, about half of which are concerned with music. One of his works alone, the *Elements of Harmony*, has come down to us almost intact. It dates at the earliest to 321 B.C., but frequently alludes to controversies in progress at a much earlier date. The date of his death is not known.

The programme Aristoxenus intended to carry out in his teachings on harmony is set forth in the following declaration:

> It is to be observed that in general the subject of our study is the question: In melody of every kind what are the natural laws according to which the voice in ascend-

ing or descending places the intervals? . . . Our subject-matter being all melody, whether vocal or instrumental, our method rests in the last resort on an appeal to the two faculties of hearing and intellect. By the former we judge the magnitudes of the intervals, by the latter we contemplate the functions of the notes. (*Harm. Elem.* II, p. 32–3)

The rule of method stated in these few lines preceded the study of the scales and the construction of what is called the 'great system' of Aristoxenus, which for centuries fixed the theoretical keyboard of Greek music. To follow out here the way in which he executed his programme would carry us far beyond the limits of our work, for two reasons. Firstly, because Aristoxenus did not belong to the Academy, the rival school to the Lyceum, or to its entourage. When he settled in Athens, the great voices of Plato, Eudoxus and Speusippus had long since been silent. Furthermore, because of the principles by which his theory of scales was dominated, mathematics no longer has a place in his *Elements of Harmony*. Aristoxenus took as his basis a tempered scale whose intervals (apart from the fundamental ones) are defined by ear; he was not worried about expressing them arithmetically. His merit rests wholly in this, that he created a logical, and relatively simple system which, for its practical utility, may be compared with the octennial calendar of Eudoxus. Only the invention of an accurate instrument for the measurement of sounds made possible—much later on—a revival of those mathematical studies which led, by way of Claudius Ptolemy, to the modern science of acoustics.

By the labours of Aristoxenus the youngest of the sciences forming the ancient quadrivium at last acquired its definitive status, after having long hesitated between empiricism and rationalism. Though less spectacular than that of astronomy, the history of harmony is none the less instructive: it shows how the Greeks learned to make the transition from pure mathematics to applied mathematics, or better, the way in which they learned to pose the question, how these two approaches—so often opposed—are related to one another.

With this last step there ended also the epoch which saw

the birth of modern mathematics. While Aristoxenus was determining the principles of harmony, Eudemus was already in course of publishing the three volumes which established the place of his epoch in history: his *History of Arithmetic*, *History of Geometry*, and *History of Astronomy*. A page had been turned. In one sense, this story was only just beginning. Euclid was at this time still a student; Archimedes, Apollonius of Perga and Aristarchus of Samos were not even born. But, as the Greek proverb wisely says: the beginning is one-half of the whole. To Plato's generation belongs the inestimable merit of having shown mathematics its true path. Theaetetus and Eudoxus are less the precursors of Fermat and Euler than their elders and guides. They not only established arithmetic and geometry on entirely new foundations, but themselves embarked on an investigation of those subjects in which, much later on, the greatest discoveries were to be achieved. That is why this generation already belongs— paradoxically—to the history of modern mathematics, rather than to its prehistory or its protohistory. Among mathematicians today, the memories of Thales and Pythagoras are certainly surrounded by a halo of prestige which is the larger because of the incontestable value of the two theories bearing their names, but justice would demand that a still greater glory should attach to the memory of those Academicians and friends of Plato who bequeathed to science a true arithmetic, a true geometry and a true astronomy. May this modest appraisal of their great achievements help to honour them as they deserve.

Index

A

Academy: foundation, 15; teaching of mathematics, 36–8
Amphinomus, 29
Amyclas of Heraclea, 40
analysis (method of), 39, 89, 102
Aratus of Soli, 128–9
Archytas of Tarentum (quoted according to Diels-Kranz, Die Fragmente der Vorsokratiker⁶, vol. I); relations with Plato, 15, 116; definition of mathematics, 20–1; researches, 40, 117, 175; the *Harmony*, 21, 173
Aristotle: classification of sciences, 33–5; astronomy, 153
Aristoxenus of Tarentum (quoted according to F. Wehrli, Die Schule des Aristoteles, vol. II): life, 185; origin of arithmetic, 43; sounds and numbers, 36, 185; *Elements of Harmony*, 36, 186
arithmetic, 23, 43
astrolabe, 142
astrology, 125, 144
astronomy: science of the calendar, 135, 144; in the modern sense, 23, 35, 124, 144, 167–8; observation, 127, 133, 147–8, 155, 167
Athenaeus of Cyzicus, 17, 40
axiom, 31, 33–4

C

calendar, 124, 134–5
Callippus of Cyzicus, 153, 166
contemplation (Greek *theoria*), 167; see also under 'theorem'
Cyzicus (school of), 87

D

Delos problem, 56, 64, 89, 114
Democritus of Abdera (quoted according to Diels-Kranz, Die Fragmente der Vorsokratiker⁶, vol. II), 19, 109
dialectic, 27, 38, 103
Dinostratus, 17, 40, 166
diorismos, 39, 107
distances (inter-planetary), 162
duplication of the cube; see under 'Delos problem'

E

element, 30
Elements (book title): by Hippocrates of Chios, 18, 63, 178; by Leon (or Leodamas of Thasos), 16, 30–3, 40, 45, 79, 102, 104, 110; by Theudius of Magnesia, 30–3, 40, 45, 90–1, 98, 120; of Arithmetic, 45; of Harmony, 177; (see also under 'Aristoxenus')